Preaching Through the Bible

1 Peter

Michael Eaton

Sovereign World

Sovereign World
PO Box 777
Tonbridge
Kent, TN11 0ZS
England

By the same author:
Ecclesiastes (Tyndale Commentary) – IVP
Living A Godly Life – Paternoster
Living Under Grace (Romans 6–7) – Paternoster
Predestination and Israel (Romans 9–11) – Paternoster
Enjoying God's Worldwide Church – Paternoster
A Theology of Encouragement – Paternoster
Applying God's Law – Paternoster
1 Samuel (Preaching Through the Bible) – Sovereign World
2 Samuel (Preaching Through the Bible) – Sovereign World
1, 2 Thessalonians (Preaching Through the Bible) – Sovereign World
Mark (Preaching Through the Bible) – Sovereign World
Genesis 1–11 (Preaching Through the Bible) – Sovereign World
Genesis 12–23 (Preaching Through the Bible) – Sovereign World
1, 2, 3 John (Focus on the Bible) – Christian Focus
Hosea (Focus on the Bible) – Christian Focus
Experiencing God – Paternoster
Joel and Amos (Preaching Through the Bible) – Sovereign World

ISBN: 1-85240-245-8

Typeset by CRB Associates, Reepham, Norfolk
Printed in Great Britain by Cox & Wyman Ltd, Reading, Berkshire

Preface

There is need of a series of biblical expositions that are especially appropriate for English-speaking preachers in the Third World. Such expositions need to be laid out in such a way that they will be useful to those who like to put their material to others in clear points. They need to avoid difficult vocabulary and advanced grammatical structures. They need to avoid European or North American illustrations. *Preaching Through the Bible* seeks to meet such a need. Although intended for an international audience, I have no doubt that their simplicity will be of interest to many first-language speakers of English as well.

These expositions are based upon the Hebrew and Greek texts. The New American Standard Version and the New International Version of the Bible are recommended for the reader but at times the expositor will simply translate the Hebrew or Greek himself. In this book I have provided my own translation.

It is not our purpose to deal with minute exegetical detail, although the commentator has to do work of this nature as part of his preliminary preparation. But just as a housewife likes to serve a good meal rather than display her pots and pans, so we are concerned with the 'good meal' of Scripture, rather than the 'pots and pans' of dictionaries, disputed interpretations and the like. Only occasionally will such matters have to be discussed. Similarly matters of 'Introduction' receive only as much attention as is necessary for the exposition to be clear. Although on the surface written simply, these expositions aim at a high level of scholarship, and attempt to put the theological and practical message of each book of the Bible in a clear and practical manner. On occasions a simple outline of some 'introductory' matters will be included, perhaps in an appendix, but the first chapter of each exposition gets into the message of Scripture as speedily as possible.

Michael A. Eaton
Nairobi

Contents

Contents

Author's Preface

1 Peter is one of two books of the New Testament that I have tended to neglect; the other is John's Gospel. Both of them I have found intimidating in their opening verses. The intricacies of 1 Peter 1:1–5 until recently left me with the feeling that I did not understand them. Add to that 1 Peter 3:19, 1 Peter 4:1 and a few other verses – and it was enough to make me feel I was not ready for 1 Peter. I have occasionally preached through it survey-style in about ten expositions or so.

However, recently a remark in a book (which said 1 Peter is 'the most consistently theological New Testament treatise on ethics') roused my interest in 1 Peter again, and I resolved to preach through it during 1997. On the first available opportunity – which happened to be Monday 30 December 1996 – at the City Hall, Nairobi, lunchtime meeting, I introduced the book. New Year's Day was a state holiday, but on the second day of the new year I started on chapter 1 verse 1, and kept preaching on 1 Peter whenever I had opportunity, within the Nairobi Chrisco churches until 16 June 97, reviewing and expanding my previous work on 1 Peter. It is those expositions that are presented here condensed into thirty-six short chapters. To different congregations in Nairobi I have been grateful for warm and responsive people: Central Church, University Church, City Hall lunchtime meetings – plus the Discipleship School at Nairobi City Hall on Monday and Thursday evenings. When I got to 1 Peter 3:13, a time of distress came into my life which sharpened my interest in 1 Peter 3:13–16 and 4:12–14 more than ever. God has ways of strengthening our eagerness to know what He is saying! For the rest of my life I believe I shall be gripped by the thought of 1 Peter 4:1 – the verse I always found so difficult.

Actually, 1 Peter was the first book of the Bible I ever heard expounded. Cyril Bridgland – my first pastor – preached through it in 'the vicarage' of Holy Trinity, Islington, shortly after I was converted to Christ as a teenager. Little did Cyril Bridgland know what he was doing. It gave me, as a fifteen-year-old teenager, a love of expository preaching that has stayed with me ever since. At about the same time I read of how Archibald Alexander used to study Scripture. E.J. Young's description of Alexander's work came to me like a voice from heaven. Alexander 'caused to be made two standing desks reaching from one end to the other of his large study. These were two stories high ... I should estimate that these stands held about fifty volumes all of them open. He would first pass down the line where the commentaries were, then go to the lexicons, then to other books; and when he was through, he would hurry to the table at which he wrote, write rapidly for a few minutes, and then return again to the books: and this he would repeat again and again, for ten or twelve hours together ...'. I was a young Christian, and there was something in the description of Alexander's work that appealed to me. As a teenager I started working on my Greek and Hebrew Testaments, modelling myself on Alexander! Cyril Bridgland was ready to give me a few lessons in Greek, for a couple of months, until he moved to Redhill. He taught me enough for me to keep going on my own until I could get more help. I knew what I wanted to do with my life. Before it had been nuclear physics that fascinated me. But now I knew it would be different. It would be J.A. Alexander's way of studying; and it would Cyril Bridgland's way of preaching through books of the Bible!

I preached my first Cyril Bridgland-type of sermon on Romans 10:9 when I was seventeen. When I heard Martyn Lloyd-Jones at about that time I added a few other strands to my ideas about preaching (and my sermons got longer!). Then with a bit of Packer and Motyer and Cornelius Van Til

10

thrown in – the direction of my life was basically set! But the beginning of it all was Cyril Bridgland preaching on 1 Peter to eager listeners in 'the vicarage'!

Most of my manuscripts are checked by Kenyan friends for comprehensibility – though sometimes they are too nice to me! This one was read by Caroleen Achieng', one of the young people in Chrisco Central church.

To Jenny Eaton, to my daughter Tina Gysling, and to other members of the family, I again express my thanks for their encouragement in the work of our Lord Jesus Christ.

To Chris Mungeam of Sovereign World, an enthusiastic promoter and encourager – many thanks also.

Michael A. Eaton
Nairobi

Chapter 1

Godly Living in Difficult Days
(1 Peter 1:1–2)

'1 Peter' is a letter written by the apostle Peter, maybe in the early AD 60s, with the purpose of encouraging Christians in Roman Asia to live a godly life. They were experiencing some sufferings and trials (see 1:6; 3:13–17; 4:12–19; 5:9) and the sufferings were likely to get worse. The letter was written while Peter was in Rome. 'Babylon' in 5:13 is a reference to the capital city of the empire, which was known for its luxury, wealth and wickedness, like the ancient empire of Babylon.

The main sections of the letter are as follows:

1:1–2	Introduction
1:3–12	Thanksgiving: The Christian's Resources
1:13–2:12	Motivations to Holiness
2:13–4:11	Detailed Instructions
4:12–5:11	Christian Suffering
5:12–14	Conclusion

In the opening lines, Peter introduces himself (1:1a), addresses himself to his readers (1:1b–2a) and gives his greeting (1:2b). The Christians in the Roman provinces mentioned in 1:1 were mainly Gentiles. The letter is a circular letter but Peter clearly knew the people well. Peter had once specially worked among Jews (Galatians 2:9) but outside of Israel there were probably no totally Jewish congregations. It was mainly Gentiles who were accepting the gospel of Jesus. So Peter is now working among churches consisting mainly of Gentiles.

1. **Consider first of all the writer, the apostle Peter**. Peter's story is well-known. He was born and grew up in Galilee. His family came from Bethsaida but at some stage Peter moved to Capernaum. He first met Jesus while they were both visiting Jerusalem. Later Peter was chosen as one of Jesus' twelve apostles. Peter was married and his mother-in-law lived in Capernaum. Jesus used the home of Peter's mother-in-law as his base in Capernaum for much of his ministry in Galilee.

Peter was the natural leader of the twelve apostles and, later, of the Jerusalem church, but he was also a man who could make some bad mistakes. He tended to make forward moves in faith only in impulsive steps.

After he had been leading the church in Jerusalem for some years, conflict with the Jerusalem authorities forced him to leave for 'another place' (Acts 12:17). I agree with those who think 'another place' in Acts 12:17 may be Rome (but the author of Acts avoids saying it so precisely). Peter made Rome his headquarters for twenty-five years (AD 42–67) until he died in the days of the emperor Nero. But he certainly was not in Rome all the time. He travelled a lot, taking his wife with him (1 Corinthians 9:5) and visiting places like Corinth and Antioch, as well as the places in Asia Minor mentioned in verse 1.

Peter was an unexceptional man in his origins. He did not come from a famous or rich family. He was not highly educated. God can transform the lives of quite ordinary people. Generally it is not the wealthy and high-born that God uses.

Peter was a changed person. He had come to experience salvation in Jesus. His life had undergone many changes since the time he first came to know Jesus. Now Peter the fisherman is Peter the apostle.

Peter was a trained man. Jesus had said 'Follow me and I will make you become a fisher of people' (Matthew 4:19). Jesus had kept His word. He had made Peter to become a man much used by God. Jesus had trained him.

Peter was a stabilized man. In his early days he had shown much instability. But the outpouring of the Spirit upon the day of Pentecost had given him greater steadiness in his life.

He had had some ups and downs, but clearly was ~~used~~ used in Roman Asia Minor and had become a ~~leader~~ leader of the church.

Peter was a called man. Jesus had powerfully brought him into doing the work of an apostle. God's calling had been at work in his life.

So he writes this letter. He says a little about himself; he is 'Peter an apostle'. But he says much more about his readers.

2. **Consider Peter's readers**. Peter addresses his Christian friends. *'Peter an apostle of Jesus Christ; to God's chosen ones, temporary residents of the Dispersion in Pontus, Galatia, Cappadocia, Asia and Bithynia* (1:1), *chosen according to the foreknowledge of God the Father, in the sanctifying work of the Spirit, ready for obedience to Jesus Christ and sprinkling with his blood. May grace and peace be given to you in increasing measure'* (1:2).

In the way in which Peter addresses his friends he is telling them something about their position as God's people. This is the Bible's way of approaching the preaching of holiness. It begins by telling Christians who they are and what has happened to them. The world talks a lot about what we must do. The Bible also gives specific instructions, but it never begins with a list of what to do and what not to do. It begins by telling us who we are. Peter describes his readers in detail because he wants to underline certain things about them which will encourage them. He wants them to know that they are able to live a godly life.

They are God's chosen ones. Literally translated, Peter's words are: 'To chosen temporary-residents of the Diaspora of Pontus...'. They are temporary residents of this world. 'Temporary-residents of the Diaspora...' is a phrase that was generally used of Jews. In the ancient world the 'Diaspora' (the 'scattering') of the Jews was well-known. Nebuchadnezzar exiled Jews to Babylon. There they were purified from their idolatry. After about seventy years it was possible for them to go back to Israel but most of them stayed scattered throughout the Persian empire and then throughout the Greek and Roman empires. Yet Peter is not referring to Jews; he is referring to Christians. God's newly restructured

'Israel' – all Christian believers – are scattered throughout the world as much as the ancient Jews were. Sometimes persecution scatters them, as happened in the early days of the church (Acts 8:2). Every Christian is a 'temporary resident'. This world is not our home, although many Christians live in it as if they were here to stay forever.

They were the objects of God's special love. He addresses them as 'God's chosen ones ... people chosen according to the foreknowledge of God ...'. God's 'knowledge' in a passage like this means God's love. God 'knows' everyone in one sense, but He 'knows' some people in a special way by His setting His love on them. 'Know' often means 'take into one's special care'. The point is not that what they would **do** was foreknown, or that their **faith** was foreknown. Rather it means that God had appointed a destiny for them because He had set His love upon them.

They had experienced the sanctifying work of the Holy Spirit. When Peter says they are 'people chosen according to the foreknowledge of God, in the sanctification of the Spirit ...', he is referring to something that happened at their conversion. God's choice of them had shown itself 'in' the sanctifying work of the Spirit that took place at their conversion to Jesus. ('Sanctifying work' refers to what happened at conversion; see how the word is used in 1 Corinthians 6:11 and Hebrews 10:10).

They had been prepared for obedience. The sanctifying work of the Spirit prepares us for obedience to Jesus. That is what Christian godliness is. It is not simply respectability or ordinary morality. It is zealous obedience towards Jesus.

Their willingness to be obedient produces in them a clean and clear conscience. Peter adds another phrase: 'for ... sprinkling with his blood'. This refers to the work of the blood of Jesus in making us feel clean. We get a conscience that feels good because we know we are forgiven and we know we are 'walking in the light'.

3. **Consider their needs.** Peter greets them (1:2b). His greatest longing for them is for a deeper experience of God's grace in their lives, and a deeper experience of God's peace.

Chapter 2

Born Again for an Inheritance
(1 Peter 1:3–4)

'Blessed be the God and Father of our Lord Jesus Christ, who according to his great mercy has caused us to be born again (1:3) *into a living hope through the resurrection of Jesus Christ from the dead, for an inheritance uncorrupted and undefiled and unfading, kept in heaven for you . . . '* (1:4).

Peter begins with a burst of praise. As in 1:1–2 he is doing two things at the same time. He wants to praise God, but he also wants these Christians in Roman Asia Minor to have a sense of who they are and what has happened to them.

1. **They have been born again**. When a person becomes a true Christian it is not just a matter of taking up some religion or adding some religious practices to one's life. The very person himself or herself is changed. The Holy Spirit is put within us. We become new people. We are not forcing ourselves to do something or dragging ourselves along to religious meetings. A new life is placed within us. We have new abilities, new inclinations, new directions, new interests. It can be summarised in one phrase: 'born again'.

God has acted 'in great mercy'. We did not deserve this gift. We deserved the exact opposite. God would have been quite just if He had abandoned us altogether. But instead He acted in mercy. 'Blessed be the God and Father of our Lord Jesus Christ . . . !'

2. **They have a living hope**. The Christian has been born again 'into a living hope'. We must realise that 'hope' has the sense of 'expectation'. It does not refer to uncertain hope. In

17

modern English if I say I 'hope' to do something it means that I am optimistic about it but I am not absolutely certain. However in the New Testament 'hope' never means 'uncertain optimism'; it means sure and confident expectation. Biblical 'hope' is expectation, prospect, future horizon, anticipation, goal.

When people are 'born again' they realise that this world is not their permanent home. It is rather the place where we get ready for our permanent home. A 'temporary resident' may be very busy but he does not completely settle down. His mind often goes to the place where he really belongs. The Christian expects soon to be somewhere else. He is looking for resurrection and reward, from Jesus and with Jesus, in a new heaven and new earth in which righteousness dwells.

3. **They are born again through the resurrection of Jesus; and they have a living hope through the resurrection of Jesus**.

The phrase 'through the resurrection of Jesus Christ' belongs to the whole phrase 'born again for a living hope'. We are born again through the resurrection of Jesus; we have a living hope through the resurrection of Jesus.

When a Christian believes in Jesus Christ, he or she is united to Jesus Christ. He is joined on to Jesus. The resurrection power of Jesus is within him. He is 'united with Him in a resurrection like His'. He is spiritually alive and is risen with Christ.

(This might make us ask the question: were Old Testament saints 'born again' if they lived before the resurrection of Jesus? It depends on what you mean by 'born again'. Old Testament believers were made spiritually alive by the Holy Spirit; and they were brought to faith by the Holy Spirit. In this sense they were 'born again'. But for the Christian, 'new birth' has more in it! 'New birth' after the resurrection of Jesus is richer than 'new birth' before the resurrection of Jesus.)

We have a 'living hope' through the resurrection of Jesus. The Christian's future 'hope' is focused on the day when he or she will be raised from the dead. Our hope is not at death (although at death we depart to be with Jesus). Our hope is focused on the Second Coming of Jesus, and the day when we shall be physically raised in glory. But this is a 'living' hope because it has happened to Jesus already and Jesus is alive! Jesus has already been raised from the dead. He already has been crowned with honour. He already has a name that is above every name. We are already raised with him spiritually. Our expectation is to be physically glorified with Him. He is alive, and we are alive in Christ. He is raised and glorified, and we expect to be raised and glorified with Him. Christians have a living expectation focused on the risen and glorified Lord Jesus Christ.

4. **The Christian is destined for an inheritance**. Peter says we have been 'born again for a living hope ... for an inheritance ... '. Or we could translate 'God ... has caused us to be born again, for a living hope *"in order that we may get an inheritance uncorrupted and undefiled and unfading ... "'*. The clause is not a clause of result ('so that we shall get'); it is a clause of purpose ('in order that we may get').[1]

Our salvation puts us in a position where we are living for inheritance. 'Inheritance' is reward. Often the word is used for our present reaping back the blessings of God's kingdom as the result of living for Jesus. Sometimes (as here) it refers to the future stage of our inheritance, our reward in heaven.

What is the inheritance? 'We do not know what we shall be' (1 John 3:2), but certainly inheritance includes honour, a name for obedience, a level of physical glory. Certainly it includes enjoyment of the glorified planet earth, the 'new heavens and new earth in which dwells righteousness'. There is variation in glory. Some will be glorified more than others. 'Inheritance' is not simply heaven; it is reward in heaven.

Our inheritance may be obtained by our living in the resurrection power of Jesus. As we live for Jesus we obtain treasure in heaven; it is 'indestructible' (unable to cease to exist), 'undefiled' (unable to lead us into sin) and 'unfading' (unable to deteriorate).

Peter gives praise to God for these great expectations! He says this inheritance is *'kept in heaven for you* (1:4), *who by the power of God are guarded through faith for a salvation ready to be revealed in the last time'* (1:5).

Our inheritance is 'kept'. We only have a taste of it now.

19

There is more to come. It is quite safe since it is in heaven beyond the reach of sin or death or the devil.

But not only is our inheritance guarded for us; we are guarded for it. God's guarding takes place through our faith. And our faith is guarded as well! Peter knew that because Jesus said to him: 'I have prayed for you that your faith does not fail' – and Jesus gets His prayers answered.

When we trust ourselves to God, He gives us total protection. His great power works on our behalf. Nothing can happen to us that is not God's plan for our lives. Even if God temporarily gives Satan a little permission to harass us (as he did in the case of Job) it will do us no ultimate harm. It certainly cannot damage our inheritance. Satan knew God had put a protective fence around Job (Job 1:10). Even when the fence was moved to a different point of Job's life, Job was being protected ('Spare his life!', Job 2:6) and eventually 'The LORD blessed the latter days of Job more than his beginning' (see Job 42:10, 12). Even if we endure Job-like experiences we are being guarded.

Footnote

[1] See W.F. Arndt and F.W. Gingrich, *A Greek–English Lexicon...* (University of Chicago, 1979), under *eis*, section 4,f, for *eis* indicating purpose.

Chapter 3

Protection Amidst Trouble
(1 Peter 1:3–9)

Can our faith fail? Yes and no. There are times when temporarily we fail to believe, and Jesus can say 'Where is your faith?' But true faith in Jesus as the Son of God and the Saviour never fails. The person born again by the Holy Spirit has been **given** faith. He may fail to apply it, but he always knows that Jesus is the Son of God, the Saviour.

The Christian's inheritance is guarded; he is guarded; ultimately even his faith is guarded! What would be the good of being guarded through faith if our faith were not guarded?

There is a final stage of salvation. It is 'ready to be revealed in the last time' (1:5). There is a stage of salvation when we are vindicated and the life we have lived is honoured. At the moment the final glory is being secretly prepared as God's people lay up treasure in heaven. One day the curtain will be drawn aside and we shall fully see and fully experience everything we have been living for.

Meanwhile there may be suffering for the Christian. Peter goes on: *'In this* [this expectation of a ready-to-be-revealed salvation] *you are rejoicing, though now for a little while you may if it is necessary have to suffer various trials* (1:6). *The purpose of this is that what is genuine in your faith (which is more precious than gold which perishes) may after it has been tested by fire be found to turn out for praise and glory and honour at the revelation of Jesus Christ'* (1:7).

1. **Trials and troubles are an inevitable part of the Christian life**. Peter's friends are already suffering. Peter is simply letting

21

them know that there is nothing surprising about the troubles they are experiencing. Any view of the Christian faith that talks as if it abolishes troubles is a defective and distorted version. There is no way of escaping troubles. 'In the world you shall have tribulation', said Jesus. He has overcome them but that does not stop the Christian from facing times of trouble and pain. Christians have genuine feelings. Trials will come. Trials are likely to be 'various'. At times they all seem to come at once! They are painful because they shake our view of God, because they undermine our self-confidence, and often there will be the added pain that comes from the fact that our friends do not understand what is happening to us.

2. **Troubles come because from time to time they are necessary for our spiritual progress**. They are not accidental. God knows exactly what He is doing. They are temporary ('now'), brief ('for a little while'), varied ('various trials'). Troubles can help us if they are received in the right way. They pull us up when we are getting careless. They perfect us. They bring us to maturity. They rebuke our slackness. They prepare us for greater experiences of God and greater usefulness in God's kingdom.

3. **Troubles rightly received have the effect of purifying our faith**. 'The purpose . . . ', says Peter 'is that what is genuine in your faith . . . may, after it has been tested by fire, be found to turn out for praise . . . '. Christians are people who have put their trust in Jesus Christ, but our faith may be a weak thing. There may be a mixture of weakness, carnality and sinful self-centredness in it. There may be much foolishness, much that we think is the Holy Spirit, which really is the flesh. Suffering sorts out what really is of 'sound quality'.

Troubles test our faith. If we pretend to believe but do not (like Judas), our so-called 'faith' will very rapidly disappear in a time of trouble. 'In time of testing they **will** fall away', said Jesus – talking about people who had heard the word of God but whose faith was a pretence (Luke 8:13).

Troubles come because from time to time they are necessary for our maturity. They purify our faith. A lot of false ideas and carnal ways fall aside when we are driven close to God by the pain of troubles. At the same time we discover how

22

faithful God is. Troubles expand our faith. They get us to learn how to lean more on God. They bring out persistence and patient faith. Gold is precious but it has to be purified to make it more precious.

4. **Troubles help us to get to our inheritance**. They do not last forever but 'for a little while'. Peter says 'for a little while' we may have to suffer various trials. These testings of faith are the very things that are working for our inheritance. God is watching how we handle troubles. They lead eventually to reward. The 'praise and glory and honour' that Peter refers to does not only come to God; we share it. It is **our** praise, **our** glory and **our** honour.

5. **Troubles do not stop us rejoicing**. Peter says: *'Even though you have not seen him, you love him. Although at this time you are not seeing him, you believe on him, and you rejoice with a joy that is unspeakable and full of glory'* (1:8). When we continue in faith despite trials and troubles, God gives us great joy. Think of the apostles when they were ill-treated (Acts 5:41).

Troubles make us live by faith more than ever. We do not see all the answers. We have to persist in trusting Jesus who is invisible to us, because He is at the right hand of the Father. But God is capable of giving us great joy when we persist in faith.

6. **Troubles do not block our salvation**. Peter says: *'As the outcome of your faith you obtain the salvation of your souls'* (1:9). No matter how painful the troubles may be, our faith anchors us to Jesus, and our salvation is sure. Our inheritance is guarded; we are guarded; our faith is guarded. Our salvation is sure.

Chapter 4

Things Angels Desire to See
(1 Peter 1:10–12)

Peter wants his friends in Roman Asia Minor to see the greatness of the glory they will experience if they lay up treasure in heaven. One way he has of getting them to see it is to remind them that the glories of final salvation were predicted by the Old Testament prophets.

1. **Old Testament prophets were enabled to predict the final glory of Jesus and His people**. Peter has been speaking of the Christian's final salvation, the occasion when Jesus will be revealed in glory and Christians will be raised to glory at the same time. Now he writes: *'Concerning this salvation the prophets who prophesied of the grace that was to be yours searched and enquired'* (1:10).

Old Testament prophets often spoke of the glory to come. They pictured a time when the earth would be covered with glory as the waters cover the sea. All things will be put under the human race. Redeemed and restored humanity will be crowned with glory and honour. Creation will be restored. Death will be swallowed up in victory. All of this was proclaimed by the Old Testament prophets. It was all a matter of God's graciousness. The prophets 'prophesied of the **grace** that was to be yours' says Peter. Final salvation is a matter of **grace**.

Peter says that the Old Testament prophets did not completely understand their own message. They 'searched and enquired' into what their own predictions meant. Their predictions were often quite miraculous. They did not always

24

understand their own message. It had come to them entirely from God, and they were sometimes perplexed as to what their message might mean.

In verse 11 Peter explains further. *'They were seeking to know what person or what sort of time was indicated by the Spirit of Christ within them, when they were predicting the sufferings appointed for Christ and the subsequent glory'* (1:11). Their ability to predict came from 'the Spirit of Christ within them'. The Holy Spirit gives gifts of revelation and illumination. He enables the Old Testament prophets to know the future. He was with them in their writing of their prophecies and predictions.

The theme of their message was the person of the coming Saviour, His sufferings and His final glory. The prophets did not only predict glory for Jesus; they predicted suffering also. Old Testament prophets often spoke of His being a suffering servant, and of experiencing reproach because of His loyalty to God. The sacrifice of the Passover lamb and the shedding of blood pointed to One who would sacrifice Himself. If Peter's friends in Roman Asia Minor are suffering at the time Peter writes, they must remember: it was always predicted that suffering precedes glory. Even the divine Messiah of Old Testament prophecy was destined to suffer before entering His glory.

2. **Old Testament prophets went through more than one stage in receiving revelations**. Peter's way of speaking implies that the prophets received revelations which they did not altogether understand. They then 'searched and enquired' and eventually God answered their enquiries and gave them further understanding. This is an important principle in understanding what God says to us. We may not understand everything the first time. God may want us to do more enquiring. The young boy Samuel heard God calling him, but he was not told everything in one step. He had to say 'Master speak; your servant is listening'. Then God would tell him more. It was a two-stage process for the prophets, and understanding God's word may well involve similar steps and stages for us.

3. **Christians may take to themselves the comfort of Old**

Testament descriptions of glory. Peter tells us of the answer the prophets received. *'It was revealed to them that they were serving not themselves but you, in the things which have now been announced to you by those who preached good news to you, through the Holy Spirit sent from heaven, things into which the angels long to look'* (1:12). The predictions of the prophets included the final glory that is to come; and it included the preliminary sufferings of Christ and His people. An answer was given to the prophet's enquiries. The final glory was not to come in their lifetime. Their writings were preparing for the future. A future age of believers would witness the coming of the Saviour that they predicted. They would enter into the sufferings that come with loyalty to Jesus, and they would need the encouragements of the prophets more even than people in the prophet's own time. This time has arrived, says Peter. The prophets predicted a coming time of sufferings-followed-by-glory. The prediction of sufferings-followed-by-glory is being experienced. Jesus has suffered. Jesus has been raised in glory, and His glory is to be revealed in due course. Now Christians are suffering. They too will be raised in glory. Their glory also will in due course be revealed. The new epoch of the fulfilment of the prophets was inaugurated by the Holy Spirit sent down from heaven in the apostolic age. Peter is encouraging his friends to understand the age of history that they in. If there are sufferings now, then there are glories to follow.

4. **The glories of the future are so great, even the angels enquire into them**. They are 'things into which the angels long to look'. The angels themselves wonderingly enquire into these amazing glories which are laid up as an inheritance for the obedient people of God. God's people can rejoice despite the sufferings. The glory ahead of them is so rich and full that the very angels admire it. Let the Christians despise the shame of sufferings and rejoice that they are given the high privilege of living for God.

Chapter 5

Preparing the Mind

(1 Peter 1:13–16)

Peter has told his readers of the greatness of their salvation. Now he gets to the main thing that is on his heart: his appeal for godliness. He begins in a fairly **general** manner. From now to 2:12 he is giving his general appeal for godliness, coming at the subject from different angles.

1 Peter 1:13–21 unfolds as follows. First of all he tells them they are to prepare their minds (1:13a); they are to face the fact that they must control themselves (1:13b); they set their hopes on the future (1:13c). Then he begins to give them reasons why they **must** be holy. The first is because of the character of God (1:14–16). Then he warns them that although God is their Father, His judgement will be impartial (1:17). The blood of Jesus Christ was intended to purify their lives (1:18–21).

Peter says: *'Therefore prepare your minds; be sober; set your hope fully upon the grace that is coming to you at the revelation of Jesus Christ'* (1:13).

1. **They must prepare their minds for action** (1:13a). God has done so much for them; 'therefore' they must now be willing to take action for God. There first thing is: 'fasten your minds'. The man of the ancient world often wore a long flapping robe. If he wanted to spring into action, he had to 'fasten his loins'. He had to get his flapping robes tied into his waist so that he could move. Peter says: fasten your minds. Get ready to think.

The word for 'mind' here (*dianoia*) comes twelve times in

the New Testament. A study of these references will let us know certain things about the mind. (i) Like every other aspect of the human personality we are born with fallen minds. The mind is controlled by the heart. The heart is the deepest recess of the human personality. People tend to be proud in 'the thoughts of their hearts' (Luke 1:51). It is not so much the mind that is wrong; it is the heart! The personality of the human person is gripped with sin. It affects everything about us including the mind. We commit sins of 'body and mind' Ephesians 2:3). The unsaved have darkened minds (Ephesians 4:18). They are 'hostile in mind' (Colossians 1:21). (ii) When we come to salvation in Jesus our minds are renewed. For the first time we begin to think straight about the things of God. God promises to put His requirements in our minds (Hebrews 8:10; 10:16). He has given us an understanding, a mind (1 John 5:20). (iii) We are to love the Lord with our minds (Matthew 22:37; Mark 12:30; Luke 10:27). (iv) Our minds must be prepared for the activity of living a godly life. This is Peter's point in 1 Peter 1:13. Peter can say in 2 Peter 3:1 'I am arousing your pure minds by way of reminder'. Having been saved their minds are now 'pure'. They need reminders.

It is a mistake to think that the Christian has to switch off his mind in order to live a godly life. On the contrary we shall need to do some hard thinking if we are to live godly lives. People who want to sin have to stop themselves from thinking.

2. **They must accept responsibility for themselves**. Peter says 'Be sober'. A drunken person is out of control. He cannot think straight, talk straight, or walk straight! But the Christian is to be under the control of the Holy Spirit. He can think straight. He can talk straight. He can walk straight. Peter says: Take control of yourself. You are not drunk. You have the ability by the Holy Spirit to get your life the way it ought to be. Get a hold of yourself and begin to live the way you ought. You can do it! The Holy Spirit is within you. You are weak but the Holy Spirit will make you strong. Don't be like a drunken man, out of control, unable to supervise what he is doing.

3. **They must take it for granted that God will give them a gracious reward at the time of the coming of Jesus**. They must set their hopes on the future. 'Set your hope fully upon the grace' – it means God's gracious blessing – 'that is coming to you at the revelation of Jesus Christ'. They will be richly rewarded. Everything they have done for Jesus will come back to them. Jesus Himself will say 'Well done'. Their honour will be visible and will last forever. It will be a gracious reward. They will not deserve it. The reward itself comes from God's graciousness, not from our deservings.

4. **They must face the reality of what God is like**. God is holy and they are seeking to be His people. He says, *'As obedient children, do not be conformed to the passions of your former ignorance . . . '* (1:14). They have been transformed into being the obedient children of God. That is what they are. That is what has happened to them. Now they must live out what has happened to them. Before they were ignorant and ruled by sinful desires. Now a change has come into their lives and they no longer need live in the way they used to. He goes on: *'but as He who called you is holy, be holy yourselves in all your conduct . . . '* (1:15). God is holy. It means He is pure, entirely separate from the wicked ways of fallen men and women. Christians are to be His people. God is far removed from ordinary human sinfulness. Christians also must be far removed from ordinary human sinfulness. They need not be removed from the people, but they must make a break with the commonplace way of living. Peter continues: *'since it is written, "You shall be holy, for I am holy"'*. Ancient Israel was called to be different. They were called by a holy God to be a holy people. The Christian is not under the details of the law but this sweeping principle is to be fulfilled by the people of God today.

Chapter 6

Bought With a Price
(1 Peter 1:17–18)

Peter has two further arguments to persuade these Christians to live godly lives.

1. **He warns them that although God is their Father, His judgement will be impartial** (1:17).

Peter says *'And since you call on a Father who judges each person impartially according to his or her works, live your lives throughout this time of being strangers here, in reverent fear'* (1:17).

God will not compromise in His judgement day. These Christians know God as their Father. They often pray to God, and when they do they call upon Him as their loving and tender Father who will hear their prayers and meet their needs. This might make them think they are heaven's favourites and that somehow they will be more lightly judged when judgement day comes. But this is not so at all. The fact that God is our Father does not mean that He will compromise in His judgement.

This judgement day will judge individuals. God 'judges each person'. It will be based on works. It is not a judgement about faith. The Christian is saved by faith only, but his reward in the last day is not a matter of 'faith only'. It is an assessment of how we have lived and what we have done.

This judgement ought to produce fear in us. We might ask: is the Christian to be afraid of God? I answer 'yes and no'. It is not a fear of eternal punishment. It is not a fear of lost salvation. But it is the knowledge that in some way we shall be repaid for how we have lived. The Bible often uses the word 'repay' (Romans 2:6; 2 Timothy 4:8, 14). We live with a healthy fear of what it will be like to be 'paid back' for the way we have lived.

This judgement ought to release us from worldliness. By worldliness I am not thinking of trivial little habits of drinking or cinema-going – or whatever. I am thinking of the fact that in one's day to day life, so many of us tend to be no different from the world.

Christians who are lazy, Christians who live for money and for comforts, Christians who defend themselves in sinful situations, Christians who are without love or compassion, Christians who pray little and do little for God – they will all suffer loss in the judgement day. I do not know exactly how it will all work. I do not believe any Christian loses his salvation in judgement day, but I do believe that 'salvation through fire' is a very fearful thing. Even for Christians it will be a fearful thing to fall into the hands of the living God. Only of those who overcome the wickedness of the world will it be said that 'they will not be hurt by the second death'. Even Christians will 'suffer loss' for every aspect of their lives which has not been pleasing to God. Even towards His own people God will show no favouritism. And in the time sequence of judgement day, Christians will be judged first (see 4:7).

2. **Peter reminds them that the blood of Jesus Christ was intended to purify their lives** (1:18–21). He says *'You know that you were redeemed from the futile behaviour inherited from your fathers, not by means of corruptible things, such as silver or gold* (1:18), *but you were redeemed by the precious blood of Christ as a lamb without blemish or spot'* (1:19).

What is 'redemption'? It is when a person is a slave or is condemned to death, but then is released by the payment of a price. It means four things. (i) Before our salvation we were in captivity. We could not break free from sin. We could not escape from the spiritual death that came as a result. (ii) Jesus Christ paid the price for our release. He wants to set us free from the power of sin and from the spiritual 'death penalty' that hangs over us. (iii) The price was the death of God's Son. He had to live a sinless life first. He could not have redeemed us if He had sinned. When God asks us not to sin, He is only asking us what He asked from His Son first. Jesus had to be 'without blemish or spot' (1:19). (iv) All who have been redeemed are owned by God. He has bought us with the blood of His Son. He was sacrificed like one of the sacrificial lambs of the Old Testament. He has put down the price not simply for the forgiveness of our sins but in order to own us. When we put our faith in Jesus, we are at the same time recognizing that Jesus has put down the price to buy us and own us.

So Peter asks us to abandon our wicked ways. He specially mentions 'futile behaviour inherited from your fathers'. Can I ask you: what aspects of your life are sinful but were inherited from your fathers? Every nation has its tribal customs, whether it is Britain or Africa, America or India, whether it is this little tribe or that little tribe – every tribe has some wicked ways. What ways are in your life that you have inherited? They are wrong but your father lived that way, and so did your grandfather.

Peter speaks of 'futile behaviour'. Much of our behaviour is 'futile'. It does no good. It gets us nowhere. It will be burnt up in judgement day as useless.

Peter says: you know all about this. You know that Jesus died to release you from those old futile ways of yours and make a new person of you. So cooperate! Let Him do it! Acknowledge that you are owned by Jesus Christ, and turn aside from every futile way that is displeasing to Jesus. Even if your father and grandfather lived that way – you be different. You have been bought by the precious blood of Jesus Christ. Let Jesus have what He has paid for.

Chapter 7

Faith in God

(1 Peter 1:20–21)

Peter is giving us reasons for holiness. One is the character of God ('You shall be holy, for I am holy'). Another is the impartiality of God; He is 'a Father who judges each person impartially'. A third motivation is that the blood of Jesus was designed to release us from futile behaviour (1:18). It is this point that Peter takes further in verses 20–21.

1. **Our salvation is part of a large-scale plan of God**. Peter says: *'He was destined before the foundation of the world but he was revealed at the end of the times for your sake'* (1:20). It is a mistake to look at salvation in a small way as if it were just a little bit of forgiveness, or a little bit of religion to add on to our lives. In fact salvation is part of a massive plan. Before the creation of the world God was 'foreknowing' – setting His heart on – His people (see 1:2) and on their Saviour (1:20). He was determining that His Son would be the sacrifice that would cover the sins of all who received Jesus and would purify their lives from futile ways.

It was planned thousands, even millions, of years ago. But it is only being fully revealed now. This means that any Christian who resists the purifying power of the blood of Jesus is setting up in opposition to something that God has been resolving to fulfil in us for millions of years! Refusal of the life of holiness is resistance to the age-long plan of God. It was planned before Jesus came; it is being made obvious now. But Christians must realise that God's plan involves their release from the profitless ways of sin.

2. **Jesus was sent to bring us to God the Father**. The way in which God's plan works is like this. Jesus is sent 'to bring us to God' (see 3:18). *'Through him you are believers in God, who raised him from the dead and gave him glory, so that your faith and hope are in God'* (1:21). Jesus brings us to God. We believe in Jesus but He leads us to the Father, so that we believe in God the Father. We would not be people in relationship with God if it were not for Jesus bringing us into this position. Jesus is the only way to make any contact with the Father (John 14:6). Without Jesus no one truly relates to God, or has true trust in God. There are plenty of people around who talk about God and think they worship God, but the only way to have any relationship with God is via Jesus. 'Through him you are believers in God...'. It is necessary to have a Mediator, an Intermediary, a Go-Between, in order to get to God. Yet it is not necessary to have a mediator to approach Jesus! We come to Jesus directly, and put our faith in Him. He leads us to the Father, and we put our trust in the Father via our knowledge of the Father through Jesus. 'Through him you are believers in God...'. It is God the Father that we relate to more than any other person of the Godhead. Although it is possible to pray to Jesus (note Acts 7:59), yet it is mainly to the Father that we pray.

3. **God put Jesus in a position where He is able to minister to us**. Peter speaks of 'God, who raised him from the dead and gave him glory...'. Jesus is the way to the Father. The Father is the One who put Jesus into the position where He is able to be our Saviour and Intercessor. God gave Him all authority and power by raising Jesus from the dead.

The Father raised Jesus from the dead. This raises new possibilities of holiness for the Christian that is drawing upon the power of a resurrected Lord Jesus Christ. Since His resurrection from the dead, all power has been given to the God-man, our Lord Jesus Christ, and He promises to be with us to the end of the age.

God 'gave him glory'. The Father put Jesus in the position of Ruler over the entire universe. From His position of King of the Cosmos, Jesus rules on our behalf. Nothing can stop Jesus' people from moving forward in God's will. No devil, no circumstance, no enemy, can prevent the Christian from growing in submission to God. Peter was writing in a situation where the Christians were being persecuted and the persecution was about to get worse. But Jesus is still king. His resources still flow from His heavenly throne.

4. **Through Jesus, the Christian lives a holy life through faith and hope in God**. God gave Jesus this glorious position 'so that your faith and hope are in God'. The Christian is one who has been brought to God by Jesus and, via Jesus, is able to go on trusting God. The Father's greatest gift for us is His love. It was He who sent Jesus in the first place. We now are able to exercise trust and confidence in Him.

We also put our hope in Him. 'Hope' is our expectation that He will be with us, that He will enable us to live for Him despite any pressures that might come from enemies and critics. 'Hope' is the sure and certain expectation that everything we do for God is preserved in some way for us and will one day be inherited. We may experience trials and troubles, but we are heirs with Christ. We are living with our sights on glory. By faith we are there, already walking in the streets of gold! We can see the new world, with the eyes of faith. We see a world shining with the glory of God, 'and its brilliance is like that of a very precious jewel' (Revelation 21:11). Our hope is set on God. Jesus has brought us to the Father, and the Father will fulfil all of His plans for us.

Chapter 8

The Imperishable Seed
(1 Peter 1:22–25)

The preaching of holiness works through a definite order. First there is what God has done for us (and Peter has said much of this in 1:1–12). Then there is the general challenge that we should commit our lives to living out what God has done for us especially in Christian love (and Peter has much to say along these lines in 1:13–2:12). Then we get to details. After that there is often extra material, clearing up problems and difficulties. This rough order can be observed throughout the New Testament teaching. Peter is still in the second stage, mentioning various encouragements to holy living: the character of God ('You shall be holy, for I am holy'), the impartiality of God ('a Father who judges ... impartially'), and the delivering power of the blood of Jesus. A fourth encouragement to help us know that we can live for God is the imperishable new birth. He has mentioned it already (1:3). It greatly encourages Christians: they have something within them that cannot be lost or shaken, an imperishable life that came to them through their response to the word of God.

1. **The greatest aspect of Christian godliness is the habit of Christian love**. Peter begins with a call to show Christian love; this is always the greatest and most sweeping way of appealing for godly living. *'Having purified your lives by obedience to the truth, ready for sincere love of the brothers and sisters, love one another intensely, from the heart'* (1:22). Peter mentions the response first ('Having purified ... by obedience ... '). This

36

self-purifying has nothing to do with baptism (despite what is sometimes suggested). The New Testament knows nothing of ceremonies that purify the heart. It is faith that purifies the heart. The purification took place by obeying the truth. When the gospel was preached and the people responded in obedience, God by His Spirit purified the heart and made new people from these former sinners. The result was that they were in a position to start loving people ('ready for sincere love'). Peter urges them to work out in practise the potential that is already within them.

2. **Peter's words imply that before our conversion our lives are unclean**. They need to be 'purified'. This is the teaching of the Bible generally. Our inner life before we get to know Jesus is polluted. Our attitudes, our motives, the generally self-centred direction of all our activites – it all has a polluting and defiling effect on our lives. We may be fairly respectable on the outside but the verdict of Jesus is that within there may be an entirely different state: 'You clean the outside of the cup and dish, but inside they are full of greed and self-indulgence' (Matthew 23:25).

3. The next stage in the progress towards godly living is that **the word comes to us**. Peter says that something happens to us through 'obedience to the truth'. 'The truth' comes to us in the preaching of God's gospel. The next verse explains further: *'You have been born anew, not by a perishable seed but by an imperishable seed, through the living and enduring word of God'* (1:23). It is the message about Jesus, the story of what God has done through Him. Jesus has come not to be ministered unto but to minister to others. Jesus has laid down His life as a ransom. Jesus has risen from the dead, and is now king of the universe. The judgement of God upon the world will come when Jesus comes again. Meanwhile all men and women everywhere are commanded to change their minds about every aspect of life and submit to Jesus as Lord and Saviour. That is 'the message', 'the word'. It was promised in the Old Testament, preached by the first generation of apostles, and is embodied in our New Testament writings, and gets continually preached by the ministers of the churches.

4. **When you embrace this 'word' it does something to you**. It changes your entire life. You are 'purified' and enlivened. You become alive in a way that you have never been alive before with a love for God. It is what Peter calls being 'born anew'. You are given a new heart, a new spirit, a new direction to your life, a new appetite. You have new abilities, new attitudes. The life of God has taken up residence in your life. The character of the disciple is started off in your life. The beginnings of the Beatitudes are created in your life: a sense of need, concern about sin, meekness, hunger for righteousness, mercy, purity, a peaceful spirit. The beginnings of that kind of life are planted within you. But only the beginnings! The new life has to be cultivated.

5. **This new life within you is an imperishable 'seed'**. *'You have been born anew, not by a perishable seed but by an imperishable seed, through the living and enduring word of God'* (1:23). This 'seed' of new life will never leave you. You will never be un-regenerated.

Peter underlines this point. The 'seed' will never be lost. For,

> *' "all flesh is like grass*
> *and its glory like the flower of grass.*
> *The grass withers,*
> *and the flower falls,* (1:24)
> *but the word of the Lord abides for ever."*
> *That word is the good news which was preached to*
> *you.'* (1:25)

6. What has to happen now is that **we grow and develop in this new life that is within us**. The word keeps on coming to you. The life is within you. You grow in grace. This is where the Bible comes in. The word of God outside of you (the Bible) activates the word of God inside of you (the new nature given in your new birth). Peter writes a letter – a tangible written document – our 1 Peter. It prompts growth in what is already within us: the new nature, the imperishable seed. It enables us to respond to Peter's call to love one another intensely, from the heart.

Chapter 9

Milk for the Mind

(1 Peter 2:1–3)

Peter now opens up what is involved in his appeal for Christian love. First there are five ingredients of love (2:1). He says: *'So put away all malice and all deceit, as well as hypocrisies, jealousies, and slanders of every kind'* (2:1). What is involved in this intense loving from the heart that he has mentioned (1:22)?

1. **Freedom from malice**. Love in the fellowship will be damaged by any kind of ill-will, the holding of grudges, the showing of hostility or hurtful attitudes.

2. **Freedom from deceit**. Good loving fellowship will shun any kind of deception or dishonesty towards each other. Cunning and stealthy ways obstruct pleasantness and rouse suspicion.

3. **Freedom from hypocrisies**. Peter uses a plural word, referring to times when the Christians might be tempted to put an outward show of spirituality that is not real. The 'hypocrite' conceals his true character or his true motives.

4. **Freedom from jealousies**. The word refers to any kind of envy of others, whether of their advantages, their popularity, their wealth or their eminence in society.

5. **Freedom from slanders of every kind**. The Christians are not to detract from the reputation of others.

These five sins he mentions are not the kind of scandalous crimes that get one into trouble with the state. He does not mention murder, theft, adultery, or any obvious crimes. What Peter has on his mind are breaches of fellowship. There are many Christians who might not be tempted to commit murder or adultery, but nevertheless do damage in the Christian fellowship by their gossipy ways or their jealous attitudes.

Next he mentions the way in which Christian godliness is to develop that which God has given us in the new birth. They are 'born again' (1:3). They do have a 'seed' of life within them created by the gospel.

1. **They are to grow in the word of God**. Like a newborn baby that instinctively is eager to be breast-fed, they must develop a hunger for the word of God. Peter is not referring to any kind of intellectualism that is hungry for 'teaching' simply as a form of intellectual entertainment. It is not the excitement of being a 'student' that inspires the Christian. Rather it is something more personal: a hunger to hear God's voice. He says: *'Like newborn babies, desire the pure milk of the word, in order that by it you may grow in salvation'* (2:2), since you have tasted that the Lord is kind (2:3).

'Of the word' is difficult to translate here. It is one word (*logikon*) which seems to have two meanings at the same time. It means 'milk for the mind', 'reasonable' milk (see the same word in Romans 12:2), milk that feeds the inner relationship to God. Yet there must also be some connection with 'the word' (*logos*) and so it is also rightly translated 'milk of the word'. 'Milk' is a metaphor for Christian teaching revealed by God. In practice it means the Bible and its being pressed upon them in the fellowship meetings of the church. We need to concentratedly meditate on the written Word of God, beginning with some of its highways (Genesis, John's Gospel, Romans, Ephesians and 1 Peter) before we get lost in the complexities of Daniel and Revelation! We need to be like the Bereans who when listening to the apostle Paul, examined the Scriptures daily 'to see whether these things were so' (Acts 17:11).

2. **They are to seek spiritual growth**. By the milk of the word they will 'grow in salvation'. They have been 'saved' in the sense that they are children of God, clothed with the righteousness of Jesus. But they need to be progressively delivered from old habits, progressively brought to be like Jesus. Peter calls it 'growing in salvation'[1]. There is more of their

salvation to be got hold of. Growth is needed as well as new experiences. Christians often want to live without much growth but under the enjoyment of new and exciting experiences. Certainly, God can give us many exciting experiences! But the 'experiences' are given to help us in spiritual growth. Christians often want 'deliverance', or 'power' or 'revival' or new spiritual gifts. All that is fine! But we must not neglect the need to steadily grow in grace. It is not growing 'into' holiness, but growing 'in' holiness. God has given us the new birth. We are alive to God. We grow 'in' what we already have, and more deeply lay hold of the salvation which God is wanting to work out in our characters.

3. **They already have the right starting-point**. They can live in this way, says Peter, because they 'have tasted that the Lord is kind'. He comes back to his constant encouragement when he reminds them again – as always – of who they are, and what has happened to them.

If they meditate on what God has already done for them, they will find many things to stimulate and encourage their moving forward with God. They have tasted that God is gracious. Jesus has died for them. They have been given the Holy Spirit. God has been willing to forgive their many stumblings and failure. They have had many experiences of the sweetness of God towards them. They have tasted and they have seen that the Lord is good (see Psalm 34:8). They have not simply believed doctrines; they have tasted God Himself in His sweetness. They have had many rich experiences of God's mercy. Now let past mercies lead on to new mercies. If God has been good to them before, God will be good to them again. God wants to be even more gracious to them, and lead them into the ways of loving godliness.

Footnote

[1] Here the Greek *eis* means 'in' rather than 'into', as in 1 Peter 5:12 where the meaning is agreed to mean 'in which you stand' (see M. Zerwick, *Biblical Greek*, Editrice Pontificia, 1990, p. 37). The blending of *en* and *eis* is specially visible in Mark, Luke and 1 Peter.

Chapter 10

Living Stones in the Living Temple
(1 Peter 2:4–8)

Peter has been giving general appeals for holiness. Now he comes to his last appeal of this nature. God's purpose is to bring into being a people with a unique and distinctive character (2:4–10). It is because of God's purpose to bring into being a holy people that he appeals to them to fight against the sinful nature and take steps to see that their behaviour is commendable in the eyes of pagan observers (2:11–12). This is Peter's last argument before he gets to some details of godly living (which start in 2:13).

In 2:4–5a the picture is of a temple; the people of God are a holy building. *'Come close to him, to that living stone, rejected by people generally but in God's sight chosen and precious'* (2:4).[1]

The Christians are to get close to Jesus, drawing near to Him in faith, and in worship. Peter uses a well-known Old Testament illustration. Jesus is a 'living stone'. He is 'living' because He is alive from the dead. He is a 'Stone' because His people are built on Him. The church of God is like a building. I do not say that it 'is' a building; but it is 'like' a building.

1. **It has a cornerstone**. The picture was well-known to Jews. It imagines builders looking at a number of possible stones. One large stone is rejected but later it turns out to be the very one that is chosen. Jesus is the Stone. The Jewish leaders were the builders. They rejected Jesus as the foundation or cornerstone, but God used Him as the foundation and cornerstone

of His Church. He is the key to God's plan ('chosen') and greatly precious to God.

2. **It has many other stones built into it**. Christians are other living stones joined on to Jesus who is the greatest Stone in the building altogether. Peter continues: *'Come and as living stones be yourselves built into a spiritual house, in order to be a holy priesthood to offer spiritual sacrifices acceptable to God through Jesus Christ'* (2:5). The Christian must cooperate with God and allow Him to place them into position as stones in His living temple, the Church.

3. **The building is a temple and has priests working within it**. Christians are the stones; but Christians are the priests also! In 2:5b the picture changes; the Christians are a company of priests offering sacrifices in the building. They are built into God's people 'in order to be a holy priesthood'. They offer sacrifices of praise, worship, self-offering, sacrificial service within God's world. Living stones are built into the temple. Priests are working in the temple.

Next in 2:6–8 there is a string of three references to the Old Testament, all of which refer to Jesus as God's 'stone'.

1. **The first reference (from Isaiah 28:16) confirms that Jesus is a cornerstone**. Peter mentioned a 'stone' before; now he makes it clear that the stone is a 'cornerstone'.

> *'Because it is contained in Scripture:*
> *"Behold, I am laying in Zion a stone, a*
>   *cornerstone, chosen and precious,*
> *and the person who believes in him will not be put*
>   *to shame."'*　　　　　　　　　　　　　　　　(2:6)

A 'cornerstone' was a large stone on the first layer of the building into which many other stones were fitted.

2. **The second reference (from Psalm 117:22) show Christ is the key to destiny**. Peter continues: *'This precious treasure, then, belongs to you who believe'* (2:7a; this line is difficult to translate [2]). He continues: *'... but for the people who are unbelieving, "The very stone which the builders rejected has become the head of the corner of the building"'* (2:7b).

Jesus is the key to rising or falling. For some Jesus is pricelessly valuable. To others He is to be rejected. Yet God uses Him as the foundation of His Church, the One who holds everyone up and holds everyone together.

3. **The third reference (from Isaiah 8:14) also shows Christ to be the key to destiny**. Peter continues: *'... and "A stone that will make people stumble, a rock that will make them fall". For they stumble because they disobey the word; to this also they were appointed'* (2:8).

The very One who saves some is the occasion of a fall for others. They disobey the word. Their stumbling is the punishment of their disobedience. When Peter says 'To this also they were appointed', it does not mean the sin is appointed; it means that the punishment is appointed. Nor was it appointed 'before the foundation of the world'. Rather it was appointed in God's many announcements in human history that disobedience to His word will bring disaster.

Peter's main point is that God is seeking to bring into being a community of people who are like a holy temple fit for God to dwell in. The pathway of holiness will involve cooperating with God in being the people that He is seeking to bring into being. Holiness is corporate as well as individual. It is not only being a consecrated person; it is participating in being a holy, living building for God to dwell in. It is sharing in the work of a holy priesthood offering spiritual sacrifices to God.

Footnotes

[1] Are these lines are commands ('Come to him ... and let yourselves be built...') or statements ('Coming to him ... even you yourselves are being built...')? The first two words of verse 5 ('...even ... yourselves') seem too heavily emphatic if the sentence is a statement. More probably, the 'and' follows naturally after an imperatival participle, in the first word of verse 4. An imperatival particle is found also in 2:18.

[2] The traditional translation is: 'To you who believe He is precious'. Strictly, Greek *he time* is the subject of the sentence. It could mean 'This honour' but there is obviously a connection with *entimon* in verse 6. The sense therefore is 'This precious treasure'. In the long run the traditional translation is right!

Chapter 11

Family – Priestood – Nation – People
(1 Peter 2:9–10)

Peter wants his Christian friends to live up to their high calling. They are God's new temple; God wants to dwell in them. They are God's priests; God wants them to offer sacrifices of worship and intercession. Now in 2:9–10 Peter confirms his description of the people of God with four other titles. *'But you are a chosen family, a royal priesthood, a holy nation, a people for God's possession, so that you may declare the wonderful deeds of him who called you out of darkness into his marvellous light'* (2:9).

1. **God's people are a chosen family**. The word that I translate 'family' means 'a clan of descendants from a common ancestor', a 'progeny', an 'offspring'. Certain clans have special characteristics. They may all have brown eyes; or they may all be tall. We recognize then as coming from a particular clan because of something characteristic of that clan. Christians are people who take after their Father. God chose us to be like Himself.

2. **God's people are a royal priesthood**. At one stage in the story of Israel God spoke of the whole of His people being a nation where every citizen was a priest. Actually in the story of Israel that did not precisely happen. Only the members of the tribe of Levi became priests. But God now wants His people to fulfil that ancient offer of Exodus 19:6. Every Christian is to offer sacrifices of worship. We offer up our very bodies as 'a living sacrifice'. We are the living temple; we are the priests; and we are the sacrifices as well! We offer

ourselves and our praises and all our activities to God in adoration and gratitude. We pray. A priest is a person who intercedes. We are priests. Unlike people in the nation of Israel we are priests and kings at the same time!

3. **God's people are a holy nation**. A nation has its own king, its own customs, its own language, its own national identity. Christians have all of these things. Our king is Jesus. Our language is our happy talk about the things of God. We love to talk about praise, about serving God, about conquering sin. This is our language every day. We have our own customs. We like to pray, to read our Bibles. We are all ambassadors telling the world what heaven is like. The outstanding 'national' characteristic of God's people is their spirituality and dedication to God! A nation!

4. **God's people are 'a people for God's own possession'**. God wants them to specially represent Him in this world. No one else does. We are the only people in this world to represent God. When people are abroad it is amazing how they like to tell people about their own nation. Often I have sat in a café in Nairobi overhearing tourists tell the waiters how wonderful their country is! Every nationality tends to boast about the good points of their home country! But our home country has good points as well, and we are to boast about them! We boast about 'the wonderful deeds' of Him who has called us 'out of darkness into his marvellous light'. We talk about our wonderful King – King Jesus. We get excited about our heavenly homeland. 'You would love it in our country', we say. Of course, I am not speaking of any earthly country but of 'the city which has foundations, whose architect and builder is God'.

What a sense of citizenship and of togetherness we should have. Our 'holiness' is not some lonely isolated, monastic sanctimonious Pharisaism. God takes us out into the world to talk about our wonderful new citizenship. *'Once you were no people but now you are God's people; once you had not received mercy but now you have received mercy'* (2:10). How desperate was our condition before God took hold of us. We were 'no people'. We had no identity as God's people. We were not specially conscious of God's working in our lives. Our lives were relatively futile; we had no sense of destiny. But now, says Peter, we are a people who have 'received mercy'. Our sins have been forgiven; God is at work in our lives. We have a sense of peace and purpose.

There is something about this passage that we ought to specially notice. These phrases in 1 Peter 2:4–10 are taking phrases that were originally written about Israel and applying them to mainly Gentile Christians. The interesting thing is that Peter does this quite casually and unself-consciously. He simply addresses these Christians as 'Israel', using descriptions of Israel taken from the Old Testament and applying them to these Christians.

What is the significance of this? It does **not** mean exactly that 'the church' has replaced Israel. It does **not** mean that Israel was simply a 'pattern' for the church, but remains everlastingly different from the church. It implies, as I see it, that the church has been grafted into God's true Israel. God's 'Israel' consists of all believers. God started with Abraham and many of his physical descendants. The first believers were Jews, and Jewish people were the starting-point of the church on the day of Pentecost. But Gentiles have been grafted into God's spiritual people 'Israel'. The church is not God's **new** Israel; the church is God's **true** Israel.

What privileges are here for all the people of God, all believers in Jesus. They are heirs to everything that was promised to Abraham. Even physical territory will be theirs for we wait for new heavens and a new earth.

The point of it all, right now, is that we live in such a way that we visibly and audibly show forth 'the wonderful deeds' of Him who has called us 'out of darkness into his marvellous light'.

Chapter 12

The Fight of Faith
(1 Peter 2:11–12)

Peter has been giving many reasons why the Christian should live in such a way that he or she glorifies God. 1 Peter 2:11–12 comes as a kind of 'bridge' section. It concludes the many reasons for godly living which Peter has put before his friends (1:12–2:10). It also prepares the way for the detailed commands of 2:13–4:11.

He has an appeal which looks **inward**: *'Beloved, I urge you as aliens and temporary residents, to abstain from fleshy lusts, which war against the soul'* (2:11). Then he has a command that looks **outward** to the pagans round about: *'Maintain good behaviour among the Gentiles . . .'* (2:12). The first command is negative: abstain. The second command is positive: maintain.

1. **He reminds them of their identity**. We are 'aliens' (foreigners, people who do not completely belong in this world); and we are 'temporary residents' (people who stay here for a short time and then move on). In practice this means that we do not settle down too much. We do not make our entire life revolve around the pleasures and pursuits that belong to this world. We are not to be excessively bothered by money-making, house-buying, luxurious holidays, time-consuming hobbies. Soon we shall be in a heavenly homeland!

2. **He reminds them of the battle that will not cease while we are in this world**. There are 'fleshy lusts, which war against the soul'. There will always be a 'fight of faith' in the Christian life until we are taken out of this world altogether. Christians that try to find a way of getting rid of the flesh altogether generally

end up teaching some heresy which pretends that they now do not sin or have abolished the flesh altogether. Any teaching which says that 'the flesh' can be abolished altogether in this life ends up in hypocrisy or depression. Peter asks us to abstain from fleshy lusts. Perhaps he has in mind sexual sins, laziness, love of ease, love of luxury, gluttony, over-indulgence in alcohol. But there are many other less 'physical' sins which arise from the fact that we still have sin in the body. One could give a whole A-to-Z of them: arrogance, boastfulness, complaining, deceit, envy, fraud, gossip, hate, impatience, jealousy, kiburi (Swahili: pride), laziness, moaning, negativism, obstinacy, prayerlessness, quarrelsomeness, resentment, spite, tale-bearing, unbelief, vindictiveness, witchcraft, eXcuses, yielding to temptation, zinaa (Swahili: sexual impurity).

These are largely sins of attitude and of our talk, but they arise out of 'the flesh', the tendency to sin that resides in our fallen bodies.

We should remember that temptation is not sin! The fact that temptations to these sins arise in us daily does not mean we are living defeated lives. We are only defeated if we give in to these sins.

We need to know that we are covered with the righteousness of Jesus Christ. If we are not aware of this 'covering right-eousness', Jesus' righteousness given to us, we shall feel unclean and unable to relate to God as our Father. When we stand before God we always need the righteousness which is not our own, the righteousness of God by the faithfulness of Jesus (see Philippians 3:9). We always need the blood of Jesus Christ. 'They overcame him by the blood of the lamb and the word of their testimony'.

When we are trusting in the covering righteousness of Jesus, we 'abstain from fleshy lusts'. We identify special problems. We do not allow ourselves to feel rejected by God. We know that Jesus sympathizes with our weaknesses. We get up speedily when we fall. We go on believing no matter how bad we feel about ourselves. We remember that our security is in the blood and righteousness of Jesus. The battle will never be over, although the front line will move forward.

3. Peter invites them to view their lives positively rather than negatively. He says *'Maintain good behaviour among the Gentiles, in order that when they speak against you as evil doers, they may glorify God in a day of visitation, because of your good works which they see'* (2:12).

It is not only fighting and abstaining. The negative is important but the positive is important as well. Not only 'abstaining' but also 'maintaining'!

We are to live a life that others can approve of. Of course they will not approve of everything! They sometimes will think we are too narrow, too rigid. They will complain about our living for God – but secretly they know that we are right to live as we do.

There are special difficulties when pagans are themselves perverse and speak against us as evil-doers. In ancient Rome, Christians were sometimes accused of being cannibals because they would talk about eating the flesh and drinking the blood of Jesus! Or they would be accused of incest because they insisted they loved their brothers and sisters! When the city of Rome caught fire in July AD 64, Nero blamed the Christians. The Christians taught that the world would end in fire (2 Peter 3:10)! In a sense we do not worry too much about what others think of us – yet we have to be sensible. The important thing is that there are 'good works which they see'. Then on a day when God is working in great blessing, the Christians' way of living will lead many to put their faith in Jesus. Some think 'a day of visitation' means the day of judgement. More likely it means a day when God is moving in special blessing, a day when it is easy to get saved, a day when God seems near (see Luke 1:68, 78; 7:16; 19:14; Acts 15:14; Hebrews 2:6).

It is these things that must be uppermost in our minds, in living the godly life. It is not just a matter of 'abstaining'; it is positively getting on with living a full life for God.

Chapter 13

Freedom
(1 Peter 2:13–17)

In 1 Peter 2:13–4:11 Peter gets down to details in his appeal
for godly living. He asks for willing submission to people
around us (2:13–17). He gives instructions to slaves (2:18–25),
to wives (3:1–6), to husbands (3:7), and then widens his
material asking for general kindness (3:8–12). He then takes
up the particular problem of unjust suffering (3:13–4:6) and
asks them to specially realise the special time in which they
live (4:7–11).

The letter almost gives the impression of ending in 4:11,
but then it seems to re-start and 4:12–5:11 specially takes
up the severe problem of suffering which is expected to get
worse.

1. **They should submit to every human creature**. They do so
out of regard for God. *'Be submissive for the Lord's sake
to every human creature, whether it be to the emperor as
the supreme ruler* (2:13) *or to officials sent through him for the
punishment of evil-doers and the praise of those who are doing
what is good'* (2:14). These verses are often taken to refer to
government authorities exclusively. It is true that Peter has in
mind the emperor and officials sent by him. Yet the opening
words are not 'Be submissive to every institution...', they are
'Be submissive to every human creature...', and Peter goes
on to mention people who have no office in government, and
he mentions fellow-Christians. The opening line should be
taken seriously. Peter is not speaking of institutions; he is
speaking of people. Every human being should be treated with

51

respect and we should be submissive to what he is and where God has put him.

In this context Peter goes on to mention government authorities. The authorities concerned might not be totally worthy of respect, but it is not done 'for the emperor's sake'; it is done 'for the Lord's sake' – that is for Jesus.

This submission includes those with delegated authority: courts, local government and minor officials must be respected as well as the Roman emperor himself.

Peter implies – although he is not as explicit as Paul in Romans 13 – that these authorities have the authority of God behind them. In verse 14 the phrase 'sent **through** him' seems to refer to God. (It is not sent **by** him – by the emperor; it is sent **through** him – coming ultimately from God.)

Peter explains the function of secular rule: it is to control evil and to promote good order. It sets up a system of punishment and reward.

2. **Living in submission to other people will eventually win approval**. Peter says: *'For living like this is God's will: doing good to silence the ignorance of foolish people'* (2:15). When Christians show obvious willingness to submit themselves to lawful authority and to treat people generally in terms of where God has put them in society – then others are impressed whether they admit it or not! Eventually they will not be able to complain.

3. **Submission does not imply loss of freedom**. Peter perhaps surprises us when he goes on to say: *'Live as free people . . .'* (2:16). Surely – one might think – submission is loss of freedom! Peter does not think so! Having said 'Be submissive', he now says 'Live as free men and women'. Freedom is not a matter of whether one does or does not obey authorities over us. It is more a matter of feeling at ease in the presence of God. Our God is a good Father. It is freedom to serve Him. He gives us freedom from fear – even under the worst tyrannies. He gives us freedom from feeling guilty, freedom from petty regulations and tiny and insignificant matters. When we love God and enjoy doing His will there is an amazing sense that we are 'doing what we like' – because what we like is doing God's will! Peter asks us to **enjoy** our freedom.

Live as free men and women! What is the good of being free if one makes no use of one's freedom. The Christian lives in the joy of the fact that there is nothing and no one to fear – except God Himself. Our sins are washed away. Forgiveness is available to us on a daily basis. Our God is not a God of petty regulations. His yoke is easy; His burden is light.

4. **Freedom does not imply license to sin**. Peter says: *'Live as free people but not as having a cloak to cover up freedom to do evil'* (2:16). One does not regard oneself as free to run wild. It is not a matter of regarding nothing as sin for us at all. This is using a good freedom to cover up a bad freedom. (In the Greek the idea of freedom comes twice: 'live as free people ... but not ... to cover up freedom ...'.)

5. **Freedom is happy behaviour towards God and people**. Peter goes on to describe this 'freedom' in a string of commands. *'Honour all men and women. Love the brothers and sisters. Fear God. Honour the emperor'* (2:17). It is really defining what the Christian's freedom consists of.

Freedom is feeling free to honour all people everywhere. The Christian knows that everyone is created in God's image. No group in society is worthless. No one is garbage or junk. Everyone is to be honoured as God's 'creature'; Peter's use of this word has a point to it.

Freedom is love within the fellowship. There is no freedom unless there are people around. Isolation is bondage, not freedom. There is no freedom unless there is love.

Freedom is fear of God. Strangely, there is no freedom unless there is fear – but it has to be fear of God. It is not that we fear eternal alienation; God holds His people forever. But we fear His disapproval; we fear not receiving from Him the honour He wishes to give us.

Freedom involves courteously and fearlessly honouring state-authorities. Peter comes back to one of his main concerns in verse 13. 'Honour the emperor'. By relating rightly to everyone and keeping a good conscience, the Christian enjoys wonderful, delightful, freedom in God.

Chapter 14

Living With Injustice
(1 Peter 2:18–21)

Next Peter comes to write about the relationship between slaves and masters.

1. We notice in this section of the letter the **virtue of submission**. This is a theme that runs through the whole of 1 Peter 2:13–3:6, and Peter applies it in three ways. It involves Christians 'submitting' to the people around us, taking note of the position in which God has put them (see 2:13). Or it involves house-servants 'submitting' to their employers (2:18). Soon Peter will say something similar to Christians wives (3:1).

Here he addresses 'house-servants' (who were invariably slaves). *'Servants, accept the authority of your masters, out of deep reverence to God, not only to good and gentle masters but also to the perverse'* (2:18).

One might want to ask: since in many parts of the world slavery is abolished do passages of Scripture like these have anything to say to us? The answer is 'Yes!' – for at least two reasons. First, if the Bible can help people in the **worst** kind of 'employment', surely its instruction will help us in easier situations. The Bible caters for the worst 'profession' that there is – slavery! If the ancient Christians could survive as slaves, surely by following the same advice we can survive anywhere!

But there is a second reason why this advice is practical. It is all very well for people in affluent countries to say 'Slavery is abolished!' – but it is really? I personally know dozens of people in more than one country whose labour conditions are about the same as that of the slavery of the ancient world. Peter's instruction is as up-to-date as tomorrow's newspaper.

Peter urges submissiveness, 'out of deep reverence to God'. As in 2:17 some words meaning 'with fear' refer to God, not to the master (see also Colossians 3:22).

2. This is obviously a difficult instruction. Who likes to be submissive to others? Certainly not me! So Peter emphasizes: **submission is pleasing to God**. Anyone can be rebellious and self-willing but it takes special grace to be respectful in an unjust situation. *'For this is excellent behaviour, if on account of conscience towards God, anyone bears griefs, suffering unjustly* (2:19). *For what sort of honour is there if you sin and get beaten for it, you endure it bravely? But if when you are doing what is good and suffering for it, you endure, this is excellent behaviour in the sight of God'* (2:20).

Peter is giving practical help in this matter. In a painfully unjust situation one must remember that quiet respect even towards the 'oppressor' is generally God's will. It is 'excellent behaviour' and God will be pleased with us. It gets 'honour' from Him.

Peter asks us to make this a matter that we take seriously. It is to be out of 'conscience towards God' that we live as we do. He reminds us that what he is speaking of is unjust treatment. It is no great virtue to be steadfast when we are suffering because of our own sins and foolishness. There is nothing so special about that!

Of course Peter is speaking generally. No one has to submit to any employer when he or she asks us to sin (see Acts 5:29). But if we resist someone with authority over us, we had best make sure it is a matter of sin. Defiance out of awkwardness or some minor opinion that we have, receives no blessing.

3. **The greatest example in this matter is Jesus Himself**. Jesus asks us to do what He has already done Himself. *'For to this endurance you have been called, because Christ also suffered for you, leaving you an example so that you might follow in his footsteps'* (2:21). Actually Jesus Himself acted as a 'house-servant' on one occasion (see John 13:5).

Endurance amidst injustice is part of the Christian's calling!

We are 'called' to it; it is part of Christian conversion. When we experience salvation it is with the purpose of becoming like Jesus, and this is the kind of life that Jesus lived.

Jesus was a human being. One might think that because we know He was divine that His sufferings were somehow not real. But this is not so. The things He suffered He felt as much as we would have done if we were in His position. When He was slandered it hurt Him as much as it would have hurt us. When His enemies were watching out to find some way of catching Him in what He said, Jesus felt the pain of it. The loneliness, the disgrace, the sense of vexation at the sheer injustice in the way He was being treated – it was all a burden to Jesus just as it would have been to us.

There was one difference. Jesus suffered 'for you', says Peter. These sufferings were part of what He had to go through in order to be a real human being. If the Son of God had never become a human being there would have been no suffering for Him. He voluntarily stepped into a position where there would inevitably be much suffering. He took the form of a servant, subjecting Himself to the will of His Father, enduring everything that was necessary for Him to save the human race.

Now, says Peter, Jesus was 'leaving you an example so that you might follow in His footsteps'. We must simply face the fact that the more we experience God's grace, the more God will get us to be like Jesus. Then we are to live in the way He lived. He 'despised the shame' (Hebrews 12:2). We do the same. We disregard any feelings of embarrassment we might have when badly treated, and we live in the way He lived, with dignity, with faith, with patience. He lived for 'the joy that was set before him'. We do the same. We live for the joy of God's saying 'Well done'.

Chapter 15

Christ in Our Place
(1 Peter 2:22–24a)

Peter is still writing about the need for house-servants to be cooperative with their masters, but his line of thought has led him to dwell upon the sufferings of Jesus. Peter says: *'He committed no sin; no deceit was found on his lips* (2:22). *When he was insulted, he did not insult the other person; when he suffered, he did not threaten, but he trusted him who judges justly'* (2:23).

1. Peter tells us **four things that Jesus did not do**: 'He committed no sin ... no deceit ... He did not revile ... He did not threaten'.

Suffering did not lead Jesus into sin. Sometimes suffering can lead us into sin. We may get resentful at the treatment we are getting and so we cast off all restraint and cease to resist temptation. In the story of Job after the account of his very great suffering, we are told 'Despite all this Job did not sin' (Job 1:22). This was a mark of Jesus' godliness also. His suffering did not lead Him into carelessness about sin.

'No deceit was found on his lips'. When someone is causing us suffering we may be tempted to lie or deceive in order to escape the suffering. Abraham is an example (see Genesis 12:11–13). To avoid a threat to his life he lied. Peter did the same in a situation where he too was likely to suffer (Matthew 26:69–74). But the sufferings of Jesus never led Him into deceit.

'When he was insulted, He did not insult the other person'. It is easy when someone insults us to get angry and begin to do

57

the very thing they are doing. At the time of His trial, and indeed throughout His life, Jesus received many insults, but never did He return insult for insult.

He did not threaten His enemies. He could have done. It would only be a few days before Jesus would be raised from the dead. He could have said, 'You wait! In three days I'll be back from the dead...!' But when He was raised from the dead He did not even bother to go to see His enemies. He could have said 'One day I'll be the judge and you will be on trial; you will be sent to hell!' But Jesus did none of these things. He did not use threats like this at all.

2. Peter tells us **the one positive thing Jesus did**: 'He trusted him who judges justly'. Suffering tests **faith**. We have to go on believing, no matter what happens to us. We remember that God is a judge and eventually He will judge righteously. We leave our cause in His hands. If we are in the wrong He will vindicate the other person; if we are ourselves being ill-treated we shall receive justice – but God must do it and it comes only in His time.

3. Next Peter tells us **how Jesus went further still in His love**. He not only did not take revenge for what we had done; He actually took away the threat of punishment by bearing the sins Himself! Not only did He endure ill-treatment and insult, He actually was being insulted in the very process of helping these sinners to salvation! Peter emphasizes the word 'Himself'. *'He himself bore our sins in his body on the tree...'* (2:24). While people were sinning against Him, He Himself was taking their sins up on to the cross and carrying them in His own body. What amazing love. While sinners were treating Him badly, He Himself was in the very act of providing salvation for them. It is 'an example' so that we 'might follow in His footsteps'. Even as people insult us we are to be willing to be helpful to them.

Jesus was willing to be reckoned a sinner. When Jesus died upon the cross, God the Father put our sins upon Him. He was reckoned to be a sinner by men and women, but He was reckoned to be a sinner by God as well! People reckoned He was a sinner – because of misunderstanding. God reckoned He was a sinner – by transferring our sins to His account.

Hanging on a tree was a sign of God's judgement. It was the most disgraceful way to die known in the ancient world. Verses in the Bible mention how hateful it is: Deuteronomy 21:23; Joshua 8:29; 10:28; 2 Samuel 4:12; 17:23; 18:10 Acts 10:39. Galatians 3:13.

Peter emphasizes the substitutionary nature of the cross. Jesus was 'substituted' in my place; He bore the anger of God against sin. In the Old Testament the worshipper who brought a sacrifice brought the animal to die instead of himself. He laid his hands upon the animal. It was a way of saying 'This is a sacrifice **for me**. This animal is about to shed its blood **for me**'.

Substitution was also obvious in the story of the Passover. The Passover lamb died instead of the sinners who were in danger when God's judgement was coming into the land of Egypt. On the cross, 'Christ our Passover' was sacrificed for us (1 Corinthians 7–8).

Jesus became a curse instead of me (2 Corinthians 5:20; Galatians 3:13); He died in my place (1 Peter 2:24), 'the righteous for the unrighteous' (1 Peter 3:18). He was offered to bear the sins of many (Hebrews 9:28).

Christ carried the sins of the entire world up on to the cross and there He bore them in His own body. God the Father executed His judgement against my sins – in Jesus. Isaiah 53:11 predicted a Servant of God who would 'bear their iniquities'. He died 'for us' (Romans 5:8); 'for all' (2 Corinthians 5:14). He gave His life a ransom 'in the place of many' (Mark 10:45). He was 'a ransom for all people' (1 Timothy 2:6).

In the midst of great ill-treatment, Jesus was doing everything that had to be done, to rescue the very people who were treating Him so badly. Jesus is our sin-bearer. So what is needed for us to experience salvation? We simply take Jesus by faith as our sin-bearer.

Chapter 16

The Suffering Saviour
(1 Peter 2:24b–25)

Jesus suffered badly at the hands of sinners, yet even while He was suffering He was bringing sinners to salvation! Peter emphasizes the word 'Himself'. *'He himself bore our sins in his body on the tree, that we might die to sin and live to God. By his wounds you have been healed* (2:24). *For you were straying like sheep, but now have returned to the Shepherd and Guardian of your souls'* (2:25).

4. Peter tells us **how Jesus' sin-bearing breaks the power of sin over us**. He bore our sins 'that we might die to sin and live to God'. This happens in more than one way. First, it involves a transfer of kingdoms. We are put into God's kingdom. It is a **legal** matter. At first, it is not a matter of feeling.

There are many aspects of salvation that involve our feelings and our experiences. The sense of forgiveness is a conscious experience. The 'Spirit of adoption' in whom we cry 'Abba, Father' is a conscious experience of the Holy Spirit. But this matter of being transferred from the kingdom of darkness and so 'dying to sin', is not at first an 'experience'. It is something that happens to us whether we are precisely aware of it or not. It is like being asleep at the time when the sun rises. The sun rises whether you feel it or not! It is like being on a train or plane travelling from one country to another. Perhaps you rest while you are on the train. You cross the border without even being aware of it. You wake up and find yourself in a different country. This is why Paul says we 'reckon' ourselves (Romans 6:11) to have died to sin and to be alive to God. The reason why we 'reckon' it is because at first it might not be something we feel. We take it by faith that sin is defeated and we are 'alive unto God'. If you have faith in Jesus Christ, you are plugged in and switched on to God's power whether you feel it or not.

But then this objective fact becomes something that we cooperate with, and so becomes an experience. We collaborate with this fact that we have died to sin. We mortify the deeds of the body, in order that we might live. We are alive to God so that we are able to 'walk in newness of life'. It is first a matter of fact, and then the fact is worked out in our experience. But believing the facts about ourselves comes first. We are 'alive to God' as a fact, then we start actually in our experience, living for God.

5. Peter tells us **how Jesus' sin-bearing provides healing**. He again emphasizes the substitutionary aspect of this matter. 'By **His** wounds **you** were healed'. Jesus was injured by the lashes that He endured from the Roman soldiers. The cords had small pieces of metal or broken bones attached to them; then the whip was used to beat the prisoner until he was badly wounded. The wounds fell on Him that they might not fall on us. The Lord Jesus Christ took my place and was lashed so that I might not suffer, was injured so that I might not be injured in God's judgement.

My sins were reckoned as His sins, so my punishment fell on Him. The result was that the anger of God against sin was lifted away from me, at the very second when I believed in Jesus. He was ill-treated so much, yet He was engaged in healing us.

This healing is not purely a matter of physical healing of bodily sicknesses. Bodily healing is nowhere mentioned in the surrounding words of Peter; it is not his theme. 1 Peter chapter 2 has only mentioned sin. The 'healing' Peter has in mind is more a matter of healing our relationship with God. It is first and foremost the healing of a broken fellowship. Jesus' healing miracles are a sign of inner healing, and a foretaste of the healing of the body at the resurrection. Of course God can heal physically at any time, but the cross first heals our relationship with God.

6. Peter tells us **how despite ill-treatment, Jesus has won us to Himself** (2:25). Even while being terribly ill-treated Jesus was putting His life down entirely for the benefit of the very human race that was ill-treating Him. Peter uses the language of Isaiah 53:6. 'You were straying like sheep'. It is sympathetic language. It stresses our foolishness rather than our wilful rebellion. You would expect Jesus to despise such folly but instead He was laying down His life to save us. The result of what He did has been gloriously successful. Now, says Peter you 'have returned to the Shepherd and Guardian of your souls'. The suffering of Jesus was not wasted. It achieved something. It was through suffering that He brought wandering sheep back; it was through suffering that He became a well-qualified 'Guardian' or 'Overseer'.

We must remember the starting-point of this paragraph in verse 18. He began with a word to house-servants and warned the Christians that suffering was likely to come for them, since the suffering Saviour is the one whose steps we shall walk in. But Peter's last line at this point reminds us that Jesus' suffering was purposeful and successful. It qualified Him to be our Saviour, our Guardian. We can expect our sufferings to have a part to play in the kingdom of God also. Since we are following in Jesus' steps we to are likely to be qualified to help others by the things that we have suffered. For house-servants – and any Christians who face ill-treatment – Peter gives the assurance that our troubles will be purposeful as were the troubles of Jesus. Added to that will be the assurance that Jesus' sufferings qualify Him now to be a sympathetic Guardian of our lives.

Chapter 17

Christian Wives

(1 Peter 3:1–4)

The next piece of more detailed instruction concerns wives (3:1–6) and husbands (3:7). Peter says more about wives (3:1–6), than he does about husbands (3:7).

There is one main instruction on both sides: *'Be in submission to your husbands ... dwell with your wives according to knowledge'* (3:1, 7). If any couple will obey these two commands, their marriage will improve. Possibly – though I am not so optimistic about this as I used to be! – if even one of them will obey these commands the marriage will come right. It does not mean that their life will necessarily be easy. It is possible to have such physical or emotional problems that – with no sin and with the best will in the world – the marriage is not perfect. But certainly a major step forward will be experienced if these commands are obeyed.

1. **Speaking to Christian wives, Peter urges submission to their husbands**. He says: *'Likewise, you wives, be submissive to your husbands ... '* (3:1). What is involved in this submission? (i) It does not mean treating the husband as if he is in the place of Christ. (ii) It does not mean that the wife does not think for herself. (iii) It does not mean that she must not seek to influence her husband – although this should be no excuse for nagging and stubborn argumentativeness. (iv) It does not mean that she must obey her husband if he asks her to do something sinful (that is, something contrary to the teaching of Scripture that both may read). (v) Submission has nothing to do with lesser intelligence or ability. In any given marriage

the wife may have more ability than the husband. (vi) It has nothing to do with timidity or seclusion in the house. (vii) It does not contradict equality of salvation, of forgiveness, or regeneration, or justification. Spiritual status in Christ is not affected by whether one is male or female. Galatians 3:28–29 does not contradict 1 Peter 3:1–6.

What then, positively, is this 'submission'? (i) It is a matter of order rather than superiority or inferiority. (ii) It is allowing the husband to be the leader of the home, the 'chairman' of discussions and plans. (iii) It is recognition of the God-given authority of the husband. (iv) It is a matter of having a gentle spirit, a respectful attitude and disposition. (v) In husband-and-wife discussions it is the recognition that after discussion has gone as far as it can go, submission is a matter of letting the husband come to a conclusion and have the last word.

It might be asked: (vi) does submission mean 'obedience', pure and simple? It ought not to come to that! In a good marriage-relationship commands-and-obedience are not the way things are done. And yet Peter is specially concerned about unconverted husbands, and he does speak of Sarah's 'obeying' Abraham (3:6). So in the final analysis, yes, submission means 'obedience'.

2. **Peter teaches that such submission will have a powerful influence**. He says *'Likewise, you wives, be submissive to your husbands, so that though some do not obey the word, they may be won without a word by the behaviour of their wives* (3:1), *when they see your reverent and pure behaviour'* (3:2). It is obvious that submission has considerable influence on the husband. Here is a husband who is disobedient to God's word. Yet Peter holds out the possibility that the wife will be able to win him over without a word, without preaching, without nagging. If submission can do this with an unconverted husband one would expect it to have even greater power with a Christian husband. Most men are powerfully influenced by feminine submissiveness. I can certainly testify that (other things being equal) any woman – wife, daughter, friend, church-member – could probably get what she wants from me if she is sweet and feminine. But aggressive

'toughness' is likely to rouse masculine resentment. 'Love must be tough'? Well, sometimes love must take tough decisions, but tough ladies are very unattractive. Sweetness will achieve more than toughness. The marriages that are happiest are not marriages with women whose toughness is directed towards their husbands! What wins over an unconverted husband, or even a Christian one in a grumpy mood? Words are not the important thing. The man can be won 'without a word', says Peter. More influential is reverent and pure behaviour. 'Reverent' means respectful of God (not specially of the husband). 'Pure' refers to general goodness of character (it is not purely a sexual matter). It would include freedom from deceit or greed for money, putting loyalty to the husband above attentiveness to other men, control of the temper, patience, responsiveness to the husband's leadership, and affection.

3. **Peter has a special word to say about external adornment**. The husband is not likely to be specially impressed with special hairdos, expensive jewelry, stunning clothes – especially if he is paying for them! *Let not your beauty be the outward adorning with braiding of hear, decoration of gold, and wearing of robes* (3:3), *but let it be the hidden person of the heart with the imperishable jewel of a gentle and quiet spirit* (3:4).

This is not a matter of legalism. I doubt whether Peter wanted Christian wives to have shabby hair, dowdy plainness, and tattered clothes. The issues are time ('braiding of hair'), expense ('decoration of gold) and pretentious vanity ('wearing of robes'). The 'hidden person of the heart' is more important than the time-consuming attractive hair arrangement. The gentle and quiet spirit is more valuable than any jewelry.

When the unconverted husband notices day after day that he has a woman who has a gentle and quiet spirit, and who sweetly and affectionately responds to him whether he is in a good mood or a bad mood – if he has any sense he will know that he has a woman worthy of being called a wife. Better still, he may want the Saviour who is her inner source of strength and power.

Chapter 18

Wives and Husbands

(1 Peter 3:4–7)

Real womanly attractiveness, says Peter, shines from within. An unsaved husband is likely to be won, not by hairdos, jewelry or clothes, so much as quietness of spirit shining through in words and deeds.

5. **Peter appeals to tradition** (3:5). Not all tradition is bad. There is a tradition among the people of God – a tradition of wifely compliance with a husband's leadership. *'So once the holy women who hoped in God used to adorn themselves and were submissive to their husbands (3:5), as Sarah obeyed Abraham, calling him "lord"! And you are now her children if you do what is right and let nothing terrify you'* (3:6).

Throughout world history, women have undoubtedly been treated badly. Even today there are places where young widows are burned to death, or where the population of women is lower than it ought to be because of the number of girl-children who are murdered, or where a woman will be discarded if she produces no sons.

The Christian faith is the only movement that has done much to change this. Generally within Christian circles, women have been well treated, and their dignity has risen. 'Feminism' arose in 'Christian' nations and then spread to other parts of the world. Today 'feminism' has tried to argue that the differences between men and women are a matter of development. (The truth seems to be that the differences are a matter of biology and psychology.) Attempts to open up every area of life to women have helped a little but have not produced far-reaching happiness. Attempts to downgrade the value of marriage have not brought benefit to anyone.

The Bible is clear. Christians should favour attempts to correct injustice and to provide opportunity for self-fulfilment – but modern feminism despite its origins in 'Christian' nations has now obviously gone much too far. The Christian church has a different tradition, revealed by God, followed by Christian women who revere God's word. It is with a gentle spirit that 'the holy women who hoped in God used to adorn themselves and were submissive to their husbands'. Where that tradition is followed it generally leads to peace and harmony. When Christian women are taught to be 'tough' or to throw off 'male dominance' – it seems not to lead to any happiness for anyone.

6. **Peter appeals to the example of Sarah** (3:6). Sarah obeyed Abraham, calling him 'lord'! Perhaps there is a touch of humour here; Sarah was laughing at the time referred to (see Genesis 18:12). Peter refers to the way in which womanly submission is culturally expressed when Sarah (maybe speaking with humour) said 'Now that I am past the age of childbearing, and "my lord" is an old man, is pleasure to come my way again?'.

Although the cultural and possibly humorous aspects of the matter can be left aside (Christian wives do not have to call their husbands 'my lord'!) – yet the underlying principle still stands. Even if Sarah was being somewhat humorous in her words, yet what gave rise to the humour was the fact that she recognised Abraham as having authority over her.

Of course there was one occasion when Sarah aggressively took the leadership in Abraham's life. 'Listen now!' she said to her husband and aggressively told Abraham to get a child through Hagar the servant-girl. 'And Abraham took Sarai's advice' (Genesis 16:2). Most of the time, it seems, Sarah treated Abraham as the head of the home and even as her 'lord'. The one exception – the Hagar incident – led to disaster. Following Sarah's one piece of feminism led Abraham into one of the biggest mistakes of his life! Instead of correcting her, he took her advice, and Ishmael was born.

However, Peter ignores Sarah's one mistake in this matter and focuses on her general life of womanly submission to Abraham. Christian women are to follow her example and avoid her mistake: *'And you are now her children if you do what is right and let nothing terrify you'* (3:6). He adds the phrase 'and let nothing terrify you'. This lets us know that there should be no fear in wifely submission. It is not timidity and fearfulness; it is bold, confident, happy, devoted loyalty. Nothing need make any woman fear – who is boldly and confidently obeying God in this matter.

7. **Peter adds a balancing word to husbands**. There is one supreme command for them also. *'Likewise you husbands, live with your wives with understanding, bestowing honour on the woman as the weaker sex, since you are joint heirs of the grace of life, in order that your prayers may not be hindered'* (3:7). Men and women are different! A husband has to learn how different his wife is from what he expects – and then live 'with understanding', accepting the fact that his wife has different needs from his own. He must remember that she is 'the weaker sex'. What does Peter mean by this phrase? Obviously it does not refer to weakness of spirituality or intelligence – or anything like that. It refers surely to 'weakness' in physical strength (we don't ask women to fight in the army). And it refers to status; all over the world women are **in point of fact** accorded a lesser status. The Christian therefore gives special honour to the one who is 'weaker' in this sense. It forbids harshness in the husbands. It condemns domineering. It encourages a spirit of care and protection.

Husbands and wives are 'heirs together of the grace of life'. An 'heir' is a person lined up for inheritance, a person about to get a gracious reward. The phrase 'grace of life', means something like 'living grace' or 'lively grace'. So it means that if the husband and wife live as they ought to live, they will experience the grace of God in a greater way than ever. It is not simply something in heaven; the reward starts even now! And if the husbands will obey this command, their prayers are more likely to be heard.

Chapter 19

Loving Life

(1 Peter 3:8–12)

Peter has been speaking about wives and husbands (3:1–7). Now he widens his appeal.

1. **He appeals for loving harmony among the Christians**. His words have reference to husbands and wives, but they relate to everyone else in the fellowship as well. *'To sum up, let all of you be harmonious, sympathetic. Show love of the brothers and sisters. Be compassionate and humble in spirit'* (3:8).

First he asks for **harmony**. 'Let all of you be harmonious'. The word 'harmonious' means 'like-minded', 'united in spirit'. It is an appeal that they will agree together to strive after loving unity.

He asks for **sympathy**. 'Let all of you be ... sympathetic' – responsive to each other's feelings and needs, tender-hearted towards each other.

He asks for **brotherliness**. 'Show love of the brothers and sisters'. They must remember that they come from a family. There may be differences of temperament among them, but they must show family-unity, family-loyalty. He asks them to show **compassion**, merciful and tender feelings towards the needs and weaknesses of others.

He asks for **humility**. 'Be ... humble in spirit'. They must not lord it over each other or be rivals in competition, with each striving for superiority over the other. They are to be like Jesus who emptied Himself and humbled Himself.

He asks for **freedom from vindictiveness**. 1 Peter 3:9 says *'Do not pay back evil for evil or insult for insult, but on the contrary*

bless the other person, for you were called to this in order that
you may inherit a blessing'. They must face the fact that they
are likely to face insult even from people who are closest to
them – he has not long been speaking of wives and husbands –
but they must deliberately and conscientiously set themselves
against any spirit of retaliation or revenge.

2. **He asks them to live for 'inheritance'.** This is one of
the major themes of the Bible. 'Inheritance' is reaping the
blessings of godliness. Christians are 'heirs' – people lined up
for inheritance, people about to get a gracious reward. Peter
has referred to this twice before (1:4; 3:7). Salvation is with a
view to inheritance. Inheritance is not justification or new
birth. It is what we are born again **for**. Christians are 'born
again … for an inheritance' (1:4). Inheritance is reaping the
blessings of godliness. It begins in this life, since those who
sow to the Spirit reap back from the Spirit. Yet it also involves
reward beyond the grave. We lay up treasure in heaven.

Inheritance comes by works of persistent faith. References
to 'inheritance' nearly always follow appeals for godly living.
Here in 1 Peter 3:7, 8–12 it comes in an appeal for godly
living. Inheritance is not 'by faith alone'; it is by 'faith and
patience' (Hebrews 6:12).

3. **Peter confirms what he says by appealing to the Old
Testament.** He quotes from Psalm 37:13–17. For,

> *'Anyone wishing to love life and to see good days,*
> *Let him restrain the tongue from evil,*
> *and the lips from speaking deceit.* (3:10)
> *Let him turn aside from evil, and let him do what*
> *is good.*
> *Let him seek peace and pursue it.* (3:11)
> *For the eyes of the* LORD *are on the righteous,*
> *and his ears are open to their request,*
> *but the face of the* LORD *is against those who do*
> *evil.'* (3:12)

He almost seems to ask a question: is there anyone who
really wants to enjoy life? Most people want to be happy but
we all tend to look for happiness in the wrong place and in the
wrong way. How then can we thoroughly love life? *'They will
scarcely brood over the days of their lives'* – says Ecclesiastes

5:20 – *'because God keeps them occupied with the joy of their hearts'*. But how can we know such joy?

Peter – following Psalm 37 – has two negative points and two positive points.

We are to restrain our talk. The happy life begins with restraining the thing that brings most destructiveness and sorrow – a wild tongue, careless lips. This is the most difficult aspect of the human personality to control. How do we do it? It is easier when we believe in the sovereignty of God! When we talk wildly it is largely because we are trying to achieve something ourselves instead of letting God do it. But we must learn not to try to shape life by wild talk.

We are to turn from evil. When God shows us that something is wrong, as He will, we deliberately and conscientiously turn from it, and put the opposite in its place. We turn from deceit and practise openness. We turn from defensiveness and leave our reputation with God. We turn from envy and deliberately find our contentment in God. We turn from vindictiveness and deliberately let the other person ill-treat us. It is painful – but it brings us liberty and release when we do it!

We are to do what is good. In every situation we find out what is the good thing to do. It will always involve loving the other person. Then we do it! It is not purely a negative life of self-restraint. It is positively and actively following God's leading and doing what is good. We are to pursue peace. We seek for ways of having peace. We will **not** compromise with sin – it is not peace at any price. But it is peace so far as it depends on us. We pursue it! This implies that peace is often running away from us! You only have to chase what is running away!

The result is wonderful. The fruit of the Spirit is love (that first!), then joy and peace and the consciousness of being in control of our lives. Then we love life; we discover that we are seeing good days. If we live in any other way, God is against us. Best of all we discover that God looks after us when we cease to look after ourselves so much. The eyes of the Lord are on the righteous, and He hears our prayers.

Chapter 20

Facing Injustice
(1 Peter 3:13)

But in much of what Peter has said there is an additional underlying problem for his friends in Pontus, Galatia, Cappadocia, and elsewhere. Many of these relationships that he has mentioned may bring suffering. The people around us may persecute us. Peter has said we may have to go through various trials (1:6–7). He has mentioned Jesus' suffering (1:11) and has warned his friends that they may have to face slander (2:12). He knows that servants may have unreasonable employers (2:18–19) and may face harsh treatment (2:20). Christ suffered leaving an example for us to follow (2:21). Peter has spoken of the way Jesus faced insult (2:23).

Husbands may be 'disobedient to the word' (3:1), and cause their wives suffering. Wives may cause their husbands much pain and distress (although the way husbands ill-treat wives and the way wives ill-treat husbands is different).

Much of what Peter has said has behind it the dilemma of unjust suffering. Sooner or later the Christian will experience injustice. Sooner or later we shall need Peter's help! There are different kinds of suffering. Christians in the western world tend to think specially of sickness or bereavement. The main kinds of suffering mentioned in the Old Testament are sickness and plagues, military defeat and what happens afterwards, natural disaster such as famine. The Psalms especially make much of oppression by enemies; Psalm 34 is an example.

The worst forms of suffering involve unjust treatment at the hands of other people. We can bear up well in a time of natural disaster. Much worse – and much more embittering – is when we face various kinds of hostility or unfairness at the hands of others. Most embittering of all is ill-treatment at the hands of those who are close to us. When the New Testament speaks of 'suffering' it is not generally thinking of sickness; it is generally thinking of ill-treatment from others.

Peter now takes up the particular problem of unjust suffering (3:13–4:6) and asks his friends to realise the special time in which they live (4:7–11). Then in 1 Peter 4:12 he will focus on the theme even more, writing a kind of appendix to his letter – on unjust suffering.

1. **The Christian does not have to feel guilty about suffering**. In considering suffering the Christian needs special discernment. The tendency of many people is to link sin and suffering too tightly. Then we feel guilty because we are suffering – or we want to make others feel guilty because of their suffering. 'If you were really obeying the Lord, this would not happen to you', we say to ourselves or to others.

It is true that suffering arises from sin, in this sense, that the fall of the human race brought about suffering. But it is not right to think that all sufferings are caused by particular sins – which Jesus denied in Luke 6:24–25; 16:19–31; 13:1–5; John 9:1–3).

The point is often made in the Old Testament that it is God who allows and controls suffering. Although Satan is involved, God controls and directs even Satan. God uses suffering to test His people (see Deuteronomy 8:2–3). Examples are found in the story of Abraham (Genesis 22 especially), the Israelites in the wilderness, and in the stories of Daniel. He puts us into situations where disobedience causes suffering and obedience enables escape from suffering.

Or God allows and controls suffering in order to discipline His people (Job 5:17; Proverbs 3:11).

Only occasionally is a particular suffering caused by a particular sin (see John 5:14; 1 Corinthians 11:30; James 5:14–18).

It is the **righteous** who suffer. Jesus was the greatest sufferer of all time. He still suffers with His people (Acts 9:4). Persecution may be God's will for us (1 Peter 3:17); it is sharing the sufferings of Christ (1 Peter 4:13). The more mature we are, the more God will asks us to endure trials and troubles for Him.

2. **Suffering cannot harm the zealous Christian in any profound sense**. Peter says *'And who is the one who can harm you, if you become zealous for what is good?'* (3:13). We tend to answer: 'plenty of people!' But deeper discernment is needed; the answer is 'no one!'

Since all that I meet
Shall work for my good,
The bitter is sweet,
the med'cine is food;
Though painful at present,
'Twill cease before long:
And then, O how pleasant
The conqueror's song!

3. **However, the 'freedom from harm' might be slow in coming**! Peter acknowledges this. *'Even if you suffer on account of righteousness . . .'*. He knows that great distress can be brought upon the Christian. He has already said 'Christ ... suffered ... leaving you an example', and he knows how severe were the sufferings of Jesus, in body and in spirit. It does not happen all the time. Peter says 'you suffer ...' and has said 'now for a little while you may if it is necessary have to suffer' (1:6). Persecution does not necessarily go on all the time; it comes and goes.

Ultimately no one can harm us. No one can affect our eternal destiny. No one can hold back the comfort of God. No one can stop the 'Spirit of glory' coming upon us (4:14).

4. **Amazingly, the Christian is to treat injustice as a blessing**! This is one of the most surprising aspects of the Christian life. We rejoice in trials and troubles. Of course we do not enjoy the troubles themselves, but we rejoice in the knowledge that it is God's appointed way of bringing much blessing into our lives. 'Count it all joy ...' says James (James 1:2). 'We rejoice

in our tribulations...' says Paul (Romans 5:3). 'You are rejoicing, though ... you ... may ... have to suffer...', says 1 Peter (1:6). We rejoice because troubles rightly received are a sign that blessing is on the way.

Chapter 21

Living With Injustice

(1 Peter 3:14b–17)

How does the Christian face injustice?

1. **Fearlessness**. Christians are not to tremble before their persecutors! *'Even if you suffer on account of righteousness, you are blessed! And do not fear them at all, and do not be disturbed'* (3:14). This is obviously something that means a lot to God. His prophets and apostles are constantly making this point. 'Do not be afraid of what they are afraid of', said Isaiah (8:12). Men and women around us live in fear of one kind of another. But the Christian is to be unmoved by the kind of things that trouble others – and unmoved when they themselves persecute us and try to make us afraid. Peter asks us to maintain total calmness. We are not to be in the slightest bit disturbed by the threats of the world.

2. **Renewed dedication**. Not only do we remain unafraid in the midst of slander and threats, we give ourselves to renewed zeal for God. Peter says: *'But in your hearts sanctify Christ as Lord...'* (3:15a).

A negative is followed by a positive: 'Do not fear ... sanctify Christ'. The Christian always goes beyond mere negatives! We are not simply restraining ourselves; we are pressing on to positive dedication and consecration to God.

To 'sanctify Christ as Lord' means that in our thinking, our attitudes, our behaviour, we regard Christ as the One who has total rights over our lives to rule, to guide, to change, to direct. Amidst troubling opposition Peter asks them to restrain fear but – more positively – to look to Jesus to be the King of their lives moment-by-moment and day-by-day.

They are to sanctify Christ as Lord 'in their hearts'. They do so truly, conscientiously, not as a matter of pretence or mere words. When the Christian fears displeasing God it delivers him from other kinds of fear. One thinks of the fearlessness of Daniel amidst a den of lions (Daniel 3:6). 'The Lord is my helper', says the Christian, 'I will not fear what people can do to me'; 'God is my refuge and strength, a very present help in trouble' (see Psalm 62).

3. **Readiness**. The Christian is not to be fearful but he or she is to be ready to speak to those who are oppressors. Peter says: *'But in your hearts sanctify Christ as Lord, being always ready to make a defense to everyone who asks you to say something about the hope that is in you. But do it with meekness and reverence'* (3:15).

Peter takes it for granted that the Christians are gripped by an expectation concerning the future. They have a hope within them, Peter says. They know that God will bless them and vindicate them any time He likes, maybe in this world, maybe after this world at the judgement-throne of Christ. When it will come is uncertain; that it will come is sure. The Christian knows that God can step in and rescue him at any moment.

Peter also takes it for granted that this expectation of God's future rewards and vindication will be obvious to others who observe the Christian. He takes it for granted that others will see how fearless the Christian is, how much he or she is expecting God to intervene in his situation, how certain he is that he need feel no guilt or timidity when others treat him badly.

So Peter knows that there will be times when neighbours ask us about what it is that gives us such confident expectation. 'You don't seem to be troubled by the way people treat you', they will say. 'You seem to be expecting that God is going to bless you, and you don't seem to be disturbed at all at the persecutions you are facing'.

At that point Peter wants his people to be ready, always prepared to give an answer to anyone and everyone who asks them to say something about the hope that is in them. 'Well, the reason is', the Christian will say, 'because I have come to have a personal knowledge of the Lord Jesus Christ. I know that He is alive. I have experienced His power in my life. I talk to Him. He talks to me. You know, He died for the sins of the world, and then God raised Him from the dead. The reason I am expecting God to bless me is that He has intervened in my life so many times before; I am expecting Him to bless me again. The Bible has many promises about what God is going to do in the future story of the world...'. And the conversation continues! But Peter says, make sure it is 'with meekness and reverence'. Don't act in a superior way to the other person.

4. **Peace of conscience**. He says: *'And keep a good conscience, so that in the thing in which you are slandered, those who revile your good behaviour in Christ may be put to shame'* (3:16). It will do little good speaking of how we expect God to bless us if we are living with a guilty conscience. We have to keep our life clean in the sight of others so that they are not in a position to slander us.

5. **Christians must be sure they suffer for good reasons not bad**. This follows from what Peter has just said. He adds: *'For it is better, if God should will it so, that you suffer for doing what is right rather than for doing what is wrong'* (3:17). We should not fear suffering too much; but we fear suffering for the wrong reason! God may wants us to suffer – in order to further His kingdom and because it is our contribution to what He is doing in the world. But, says Peter, let us make sure it is for God that we are suffering and not for our own sinfulness or foolishness.

Chapter 22

Victory After Suffering

(1 Peter 3:16–18)

Amidst unjust sufferings, Christians must be: ready (3:15), conscientiousness (3:16), making sure we suffer for good reasons (3:17). Jesus' atonement also involved unjust suffering (3:18). Indeed Jesus is the classic example of God's purpose going forward through unjust suffering.

Peter reminds us again that Jesus' sufferings also involved unjust suffering (3:18). His death was a substitutionary atonement. It leads to our death to sin, our rising to newness of life.

'For Christ also suffered for sins once for ever, the righteous one in the place of unrighteous people, in order to bring us to God, having been put to death in the flesh, but made alive by the Spirit' (3:18).

Jesus' death upon the cross is the outstanding proof that sufferings are purposeful. When Christians suffer injustice, it is because they are following in the footsteps of Jesus. God's plan for saving the world involved sufferings in the life of Jesus. God's plans for using His people in this world involve their sufferings also. Although the sufferings of the people of God are not atoning sufferings, yet they are necessary for God to fulfil His purpose. This is a mysterious matter, yet there can be no doubt that the purpose of God goes forward as we endure trials and tribulations for the sake of Jesus, just as the purpose of God went forward when Jesus suffered. For this reason the Christian in his own suffering, gets encouragement by seeing what God achieved in Jesus' sufferings.

1. **Jesus' death upon the cross was 'for sins'**. The human race had a bad problem because of sin. Sin brings guilt, punishment, and pollution. It damages our relationship with God, with others, with ourselves. But Jesus died 'for sins'. He sacrificed Himself, in order to bring forgiveness and restoration.

2. **Jesus' death upon the cross was a completed work**. Jesus died 'once for ever' (compare Romans 6:10; Hebrews 7:27; 9:22, 26, 28; 10:10). There will never be any need of another sacrifice for sins. All other atoning sacrifices are overshadowed and needless. Jesus never needs to die for us again, because He offered Himself for sins 'once for ever'.

3. **Jesus' death upon the cross was a work of substitution**. He died 'the righteous person in the place of unrighteous people'. The sins of the entire human race were placed upon Him, and He bore the penalty and punishment for them. He was punished where we should have been punished. He was wounded for our transgressions; He was bruised for our iniquities. The Lord laid on Him the iniquity of us all.

4. **Jesus' death upon the cross was designed to restore us to fellowship with God**. He died 'to bring us to God'. When sin was removed out of the way so as to be no longer a barrier between man and God, the possibility of reconciliation and harmony with God was opened up for us. Jesus' death brings us to God ready to praise Him, ready to serve Him.

Again, Peter insists that Jesus' sufferings were purposeful. Because of the sacrifice of Jesus upon the cross, God's people now know God. Sin was the barrier between us and God. Now – through Jesus' sacrifice upon the cross – it may be forgiven and so we have been 'brought to God'. God could only be displeased with us, at the time when sins were heavy upon us. But Jesus has died! We have believed! The sacrifice of the cross has been applied to us! So we have been brought to God. God is our Father. Jesus is our Saviour and Friend. The Holy Spirit is our Guide and Sustainer. The blood of Jesus Christ has brought us to God.

5. **Jesus' death upon the cross was followed up by vindication and victory**. Having been 'put to death in the flesh' He was 'made alive by the Spirit'.

It must be noted that Peter does not say 'being kept alive in the spirit' or 'remaining alive in His spirit'. Peter is not referring to body-and-spirit and then referring what happens to 'the spirit'. That is not Peter's point.

Rather Peter uses the word 'made alive'. It is a reference to the resurrection of Jesus. The Holy Spirit was at work in the resurrection of Jesus. The Spirit is 'the Spirit of him who raised Jesus from the dead' (Romans 8:13). The thought of 1 Peter 3:18 is similar to the thought in Romans 1:3–4 and 1 Timothy 3:16, in both of which there is probably a reference to the Holy Spirit.

When Jesus died, He died 'in the flesh'. They ill-treated him physically. His human weakness was very obvious. The Father did not send twelve legions of angels to rescue Him and His eleven faithful apostles. The weakness of human nature was very conspicuous.

When Jesus was made alive, He was raised by the power of the Holy Spirit. The Spirit reversed the judgement of the court of Pontius Pilate. Jesus was given a transformed body and was able to say 'All power has been given unto Me'. He was crucified in weakness but raised by the power of God.

Peter is saying all of this – it must be remembered – to encourage Christians who are suffering. Jesus' death and resurrection is the classic proof that sufferings do not defeat God; they accomplish His purposes and they issue in triumph.

If the terrible sufferings of Jesus were reversed by God, if the weakness of the flesh was followed by the power of the Spirit – then the Christians can expect the same thing to happen to them. They may be in the midst of severe trials, but God knows what He is doing. Suffering for righteousness' sake achieves something in the kingdom of God, and then is followed by vindication. This is what happened to Jesus; this is what will happen to us.

Chapter 23

The Spirits in Prison
(1 Peter 3:19–20)

1 Peter 3:19–22 are famous for their difficulty, and famous for the strange ideas that have been read into them!

We must remember the flow of the argument. Christians are to be peaceable. Ultimately they will not suffer (3:13). Suffering for righteousness' sake brings God's blessing (3:14). Meanwhile we must be ready to explain ourselves to unconverted people (3:15). We must be conscientiousness (3:16), making sure we suffer persecution only for good reasons (3:17). Jesus' atonement also involved unjust suffering (3:18), says Peter. Indeed Jesus is the classic example of God's purpose going forward through unjust suffering. His death was a substitution. It leads to our death to sin. It leads ultimately to victory.

It is this last matter which is the main point of 1 Peter 3:19–20. The unjust suffering of Jesus did not lead to failure; it led to the greatest triumph imaginable. Jesus' death led to His victory. Peter's friends need to remember this. After Jesus rose from the dead He went to proclaim His triumph to the most notorious group of evil spirits ever known in the history of the world (3:19–20).

'In the Spirit also he went and made a proclamation to the spirits in prison (3:19). These were the ones who were disobedient at the time when the patience of God was waiting during the days when Noah was building the ark, in which a few, that is eight people, were rescued through water' (3:20).

Some points of interpretation need to be mentioned. (i) I

take it that it is certain that 'made alive in the Spirit' (3:18) refers to the resurrection. So 3:19 does not (in my opinion) refer to the time between Jesus' death and resurrection. Nor does it refer to the pre-existent Christ in the days of Noah. (ii) The first two Greek words of verse 19 ('in which') refer to the Holy Spirit ('In the Spirit') or to the whole idea just mentioned ('In the state of being made alive in the Spirit'); the difference is not great. Either way the event mentioned here was achieved by the Lord Jesus Christ. (iii) The 'spirits' are the evil spirits involved in the sin at the time of the flood. They are not human beings.[1] (iv) 'Made a proclamation' does not refer to preaching the gospel; it refers to a more general 'proclamation'. Colossians 2:15 gives a hint of the nature of the proclamation. Peter does not here use the word 'preach good news', which he uses elsewhere (1:12, 25; 4:6). (v) 'Prison' refers to the temporary holding place in which spirits are held until a time of punishment (compare Revelation 20; 2 Peter 2:4; Jude 6). (vi) Although the location of the prison is not mentioned, it is more likely that the 'going' is part of Jesus' ascension (note the 'going' into heaven in 3:22 where the same word is used). If the question is asked, the 'going' is going up, not going down! There was a triumphant victory over evil spirits in the cross; the ascension was Jesus triumphant 'going' to a place of supreme kingship (see 3:22).

1.**Christians need to be aware they are in a spiritual battle**. Peter and his friends are living in extremely difficult days. There is much evil around. Many pagans are 'disobedient' to God (2:4, 8). Behind the threatening situation is the activity of Satan (as 1 Peter 5:8 will say). The situation was similar in Noah's days. While Noah was building the ark, he and his family were a tiny minority facing an ungodly environment.

2. **The continuance of the persecutors is another example of the slowness of God to judge wickedness**. God was patient in the days of the flood. The wickedness of those days had wicked spirits behind them; so it is in Peter's day also. But they need not worry, Jesus will triumph again, because He has triumphed already. The continuance of opposition is not God's failure; it is God's patience.

3. **Their unjust suffering will lead them into ultimate triumph.**

Just as Jesus triumphed over the evil powers behind this world, so will the Christians. Peter and his friends might well suffer, but they should know that suffering is a highway that leads to triumph, even over the forces of wickedness.

The sufferings of these friends of Peter must not make them lose heart. The greatest persecution of all history was perhaps that experienced by Noah, when eight people were faced by the ridicule of the entire Mesopotamian world! The judgement was slow in coming but eventually the wicked generation of Noah's day were swept away. Peter's friends are likewise in a hostile environment. Jesus was crucified and anything might happen to His disciples. (We recall that Peter himself would – as the earliest Christian history book tells us – be crucified in Rome, 'crucified head downwards, for this is how he requested to suffer'.[2])

Yet despite the terrible opposition that Noah must have faced, he was brought through to safety. When the judgement fell, Noah and his tiny 'congregation' were kept safe: 'a few ... were saved, rescued, brought to safety, through water'. The Christians of Roman Asia Minor can be sure something similar will happen to them. Jesus has triumphed over the evil spirits; He is at the right hand of the Father. No matter what happens, Peter and his friends will be triumphant.

Footnotes

[1] There is no example of the word 'spirit' (without a following 'of...') referring to a human being. When a human being is referred to there is a following 'of...' (as in Hebrews 12:23, the only example in the New Testament). 'Spirits' in the New Testament mainly refers to evil spirits. The story that Peter refers to was famous among first century Jews. The Ethiopic book of Enoch (1 Enoch 10–16; 21 especially) is one of several Jewish documents which give us the background to 1 Peter 3:19–20; see 1 Enoch in J.H. Charlesworth, *Old Testament Pseudepigrapha* (Doubleday, 1983), which contains also 2 Baruch 56:12; Testament of Naphtali 3:5 and 2 Enoch 7:1–3.

[2] See Eusebius, *Ecclesiastical History*, 2:25:5–8; 3:1:2.

Chapter 24

An Appeal for a Good Conscience

(1 Peter 3:21–22)

Eight people were rescued through water, says Peter. The first Greek words of verse 21 may be translated 'which also ...'. The 'which' refers to 'water' mentioned in verse 20. We may translate: 'This water ... also ...'.

'This water – which is an illustration of baptism – now saves us also, not as a putting away of filth from the sinful nature, but as an appeal for a good conscience through the resurrection of Jesus Christ' (3:21).

At the time of the flood, Noah and his family were 'saved through water'. The phrase in verse 21 is nicely ambiguous! The Greek 'through' means both 'through' in the sense of a change of location, and 'through' in the sense of 'by means of'. Noah and his family were brought to safety through the flood-waters that drowned the Mesopotamians. At the same time, because they were in the ark, it was the water itself which lifted them up above the doomed world around them. They were brought safely 'through' the water; and the water that drowned others lifted them to safety. They were brought to safety by means of the water! The element that caused the destruction also caused the salvation!

All of this, Peter says, is an 'illustration' of what happens when a person comes to salvation in Jesus and is baptized. The Christian's baptism may be used by God to lift him up above the waves of sin, guilt and condemnation. When water-baptism is rightly used with faith, much spiritual blessing may come. The flood-waters lifted the small family to safety above the drowning world beneath them. Something similar may happen in water-baptism.

1. **Peter explicitly denies any doctrine of salvation-by-ceremony**. He denies that water-baptism has any direct power to cleanse the sinful nature of men and women. He explicitly says: it is not a putting away of filth from the sinful nature. I do not think that Peter's point is that water-baptism does not save us as an **ordinary** washing of the body. Surely Peter is saying something deeper and more profound than that! 'Flesh' here surely refers to 'sinful nature' as often in Paul's writings (see Galatians 5:16, 17), in John's writings (see John 3:5) and in 2 Peter 2:10, 18; Jude 23. The phrase 'filth of the flesh' makes is certain that 'flesh' has the meaning 'sinful nature' in 1 Peter 3:21. Water-baptism has no direct action in cleansing the sinful nature. Any doctrine of salvation-by-ceremony must be firmly rejected. There is no grace in the water of baptism!

For some expositors, water-baptism (provided that there is no wilful resistance) achieves the eradication of original sin, the eradication of all personal sins, and the impartation of a new spiritual nature – even in newborn infants! But there are millions of 'water-baptised' people, perhaps sprinkled in infancy, who in no way show any evidence whatsoever of having a new nature. What sort of 'regeneration' is it that has not the slightest effect upon the life and character of the person concerned? Any such 'baptismal regeneration' must be a very useless, ineffective 'regeneration' indeed! On the contrary, 'new birth' comes directly from God (see 1:3), takes effect through God's word (see 1:22–25) and endures forever! The administration of water does not in itself bring about any new birth. In fact, nothing physical or material brings a new nature into the heart of man or effects any new birth.

The preoccupation of the church with baptism as a means of new birth stems from the superstition about water that gripped the church as early as the second century. Very early in the church Christians fell into superstition about baptismal water. Justin Martyr in the second century thought the administration of water gave 'power to regenerate'.[1] For Irenaeus in the second century, water-baptism **is** 'rebirth unto

God'.[2] Tertullian at about the same time said 'Nobody can be saved without baptism'.[3] But if this refers to the administration of water, it is simply superstition – as a little reflection on Acts 10:47 will reveal. The early church tended towards superstition at this point; it has affected the church ever since.

2. **Water-baptism is an expression of faith**. Peter explains how baptism can be a means of 'saving' us, lifting us above judgement. It does so because it may be 'an appeal[4] for a good conscience through the resurrection of Jesus Christ'. Baptism is a way of publicly expressing faith in Jesus. The baptized person is declaring his faith, and calling upon God for a conscious experience of forgiveness. The baptized person is already right with God, but is looking for a conscious experience of forgiveness. He wants a good conscience. He or she wants to feel forgiven and clean by the Holy Spirit.

3. **Water-baptism is a prayer**. The baptized person is believing God's promises and calling upon God for a good conscience; so baptism is a kind of prayer. Acts 22:16 illustrates Peter's point. Saul of Tarsus had already come to faith in Jesus; he was already 'justified', right with God. 'Rise and be baptised, and wash away your sins, calling on his name'. Paul was already a child of God. He is now to be baptized – and to use his baptism as an occasion to appeal to God for a good conscience! He must call on the name of the Lord. God will hear his prayers and his conscience will be cleansed from any sense of guilt. He will feel forgiven.

Acts 2:38 also illustrates Peter's point. The crowd in Jerusalem had already come to faith (as verse 37 shows). They are ready to do anything God asks of them. Peter tells them to express their faith by being baptized. The result will be a sense of forgiveness, and the outpouring of the Spirit upon them, sealing their salvation.

Just as Noah's family went through water into a new world, so faith in Jesus expressed in baptism brings us into a new world also! Baptism does not save us from 'the flesh' as if baptism were a magic power. Rather it is an expression of faith looking for the experience of God's forgiveness.

Next Peter goes a step further. The 'ark' of salvation is not a boat; it is Jesus Himself at the right hand of God. *'He is at* the right hand of God, having gone into heaven, having subjected to himself angels and authorities and powers' (3:22). Noah was rescued by walking into a boat. The Christian is lifted up above the feeling of guilt by putting his faith in Jesus, and expressing that faith in water-baptism. God is then likely to pour out the Spirit upon him and 'seal' to him in his conscience, the forgiveness of sins.

The last phrase of verse 22 confirms our interpretation of 3:19. Jesus has made a journey into heaven. In doing so He has conquered all spiritual powers. 1 Peter 3:22 confirms 3:19. The risen Lord Jesus Christ has died for our sins; His sacrifice has been accepted to give us freedom from guilt. When we get baptized we appeal for a good conscience through the resurrection of Jesus Christ.

Footnotes

[1] *Adversus Omnes Haereses* 3:17:2.
[2] *Proof of the Apostolic Preaching*, 3.
[3] *De Bapt.* 12:1.
[4] One meaning of *eperotao* is 'to request, to appeal'; I take it that *eperotema* has a related meaning.

Chapter 25

Breaking With Sin
(1 Peter 4:1–3)

Peter is still dealing with the Christian's experience of unjust suffering. Jesus suffered unjustly but it led to His triumph. The subject continues in 1 Peter chapter 4.

'*Therefore, now that Christ has suffered in the flesh, arm yourself also with the same thought – the thought that he who has suffered in the flesh has ceased from sin . . .*' (4:1). The word 'therefore' links 1 Peter 4:1 with 3:18–22.

1. **Jesus adopted a certain attitude towards sin and suffering when He died upon the cross**.

'Suffered in the flesh' refers to Jesus' death on the cross. The tense of the verb refers to an event on a definite occasion; it is the same tense used in 1 Peter 3:18.

Why was Jesus willing to endure such disgrace and suffering? He went to the cross with a certain 'mentality'. We know that He was willing to humble Himself. This was 'the mind of Christ' as He obeyed His Father (see Philippians 2:5–8). We know that He was looking forward to the joy of being rewarded by His Father; this helped Him to despise the shame and endure the cross (see Hebrews 12:2). He was dealing a death-blow to sin. He was condemning it (Romans 8:3), buying our freedom from it (Mark 10:45). As a result Jesus utterly conquered it and finished with it forever. He has 'died to sin', never to come under its influence again (as Romans 6:10 has it). This was His 'thought' or 'purpose' from the beginning. Jesus knew that He was to be a ransom for sin. He steadfastly set out to go to the cross (Luke 9:51). He knew

89

that it would involve extreme suffering for Him, and He would have preferred to avoid suffering if it were possible. But He also knew He would utterly conquer sin and Satan by obeying the Father.

He knew that when He had suffered, His relationship to sin would be finished. He would no longer be the Sin-bearer. All angels and authorities and powers would be subject to Him.

Jesus is the classic example of God's purpose going forward through unjust suffering. His death leads to our death to sin. The baptized person is declaring his faith. Just as Noah's family went through water into a new world, so faith in Jesus expressed in baptism brings us into a new world also!

2. **The Christian approaches sin armed with the same mentality**. Jesus' suffering on the cross was an indication of His determination and willingness to suffer in order to conquer the entire realm and kingdom of sin. Now, says Peter to his Christian friends, ' ... *arm yourself also with the same thought* ... '. This seems to mean two things: (i) arm yourself with the thought that Christ's having suffered has taken Him into a realm of victory. You are 'in Christ', so you are in a realm of victory also – in Christ. (ii) But there is a second strand in what it means to 'arm yourself also with the same thought'. It surely includes the idea that we should follow Jesus' example. If Jesus' willingness to suffer led to His death upon the cross, and to His achieving a decisive victory over sin, surely something analogous and similar can be true in our lives also. If He has conquered sin, in the first place, we may conquer sin as people who follow on after what Jesus has done.

Christ has died to sin; we die to sin in Christ. But them Romans 6 says 'Do not let sin reign in your bodies' (see Romans 6:12). The power of sin has been broken – so break its power even more!

1 Peter 4:1 is analogous. Jesus has finished with sin-bearing and has been transferred to another realm; we have ceased from sin because we are 'in Christ'; so now we cease from sin even more!

Two items of interpretation are involved in this exposition; they seem to be necessary for verse 1 to make sense. (i) The eleventh word in the Greek sentence means 'that' (not 'because'). (ii) Verse 1a ('he who has suffered ... has ceased from sin') refers to Jesus.

The Christian 'arms' himself with the same mentality that Jesus had. He has been transferred to a realm of righteousness. Now, like Jesus, he faces the future with a firm determination that he or she will conquer sin. Jesus has already dealt it a deathblow and broken its power over him. Now he or she also is 'armed' with the same purpose and mentality.

Peter's words imply that the Christian is conscious of being in a fight. Sin is defeated – but sin does not surrender easily. It fights back. It fights to overcome us again. **A person who is willing to suffer in order to defeat sin is a person with a powerful piece of weaponry!** Jesus went to the cross with this mentality; the Christian faces pressures to sin with the same attitude. Jesus was willing to lay down His life rather than fail to defeat sin. The Christian who feels the same way is in a powerful position; he is powerfully 'armed'.

3. **The Christian faces the future with a firm resolve that the sins of the past will be left aside**. Peter goes on to say: *'Arm yourself also with the same thought – the thought that he who has suffered in the flesh has ceased from sin – in order to live the remaining time in the flesh no longer in human lusts but in the will of God'* (4:2). From now on the Christian will face any suffering rather than disobey God's will. Although given much freedom, the Christian knows that God has wishes and purposes. The Christian is free but he wants to please God. *'For the time that has gone by is sufficient to have accomplished the desire of the Gentiles, to have walked in the ways of sensuality, in immoral desires, in drunkenness, revelry, drinking-parties, and the indecent practices of idolatry'* (4:3). These Christians in Roman Asia Minor had indulged in this kind of wild living, but now Peter wants them to say 'Never again! I have had more than enough of the life of sin. From now on I shall live for God, no matter what happens to me'.

Chapter 26

The Christians' Final Vindication
(1 Peter 4:4–6)

The Christian is willing to suffer. He has broken with sin. He denounces his past wickedness. Now he surprises and annoys his pagan neighbours (4:4). But these pagan neighbours will stand before God in the judgement day and give an account to God of their hostility to Christians (4:5). Everyone will face God's judgement; He will judge 'the living and the dead'.

1. **The grace of God is always surprising; it surprises the Christians themselves and it vexes the ungodly**. Peter says *'In this matter they find it strange that you do not now join them in the same wild profligacy; and so they slander you'* (4:4). When a person comes to a personal knowledge of Jesus as Saviour, he or she becomes unwilling to join in with the pagan amusements of their onetime friends and colleagues. They now want to avoid pagan life with its immoralities, its drunkenness and its idolatry. The Christians' former friends are at first astonished, but soon their astonishment turns to hostility.

Christians find that the more they sincerely live for the honour of God, the more their devotion to God arouses bitterness and resentment. Slander is yet one more form of persecution that the Christian may have to face. There is plenty of evidence that Christians were accused of all sorts of vicious crimes. They were accused of being law-breakers, of believing deadly superstitions, of being magicians worthy of severe punishment. Peter himself writes from Rome where not long after he wrote this letter, Christians would be accused of causing the Great Fire of Rome in AD 64. The

Christians refused to rush into the same wild living as their pagan neighbours. Hostility and slander were the result.

2. **Peter encourages the Christians with the thought that God's judgement day will be a reply to all injustices**. Those who abuse and insult Christians out of resentment and animosity will find that one day their injustices and slanders will be corrected. Peter says: *'They will give an account to the one who is ready to judge the living and the dead'* (4:5).

Christians may face slander now, but one day the record will be put straight. The **facts** will be exposed. The **truth** will come out. The **motives** will be revealed. One day we shall know why everyone did what he or she did. The **causes and circumstances** will be brought to light. We shall discover what sins arose from sincere mistakes and misunderstanding, and what slanders arose from hostility and a desire to interpret the other person in the worst possible light. Those who slander God's people will have to give an account of every idle word. The thoughts and secrets of their hearts will be exposed.

Then **retribution and reward** will be allocated. The slanderer will in some way be repaid for what he or she has done. The Christian will be vindicated; every word spoken for Jesus shall be rewarded. Every piece of suffering endured for Jesus will receive compensation, in some way unknown to us.

3. **God's judgement will involve 'the living' (those who are alive at the time of Jesus' coming) and 'the dead' (those who have died at the time of Jesus' coming)**. Praise and blame, penalty or reward, will come to everyone. God will decide the eternal destiny of those who have ill-treated His people; He will make decisions concerning the honour and reward for His own people who have suffered for Jesus' sake.

Verse 6 follows on quite naturally from this point. God will judge the living and the dead, *'For this is why the gospel was preached also to the dead, that though in the flesh they might be condemned in the eyes of men and women, by the Spirit they will experience life, in accordance with the decision of God'* (4:6).

The point of the sentence is: **even death will not stop heavenly reward coming to the persecuted Christian**. God will allocate justice to those who are alive and also to those who have died, at the time of Jesus' coming. Verse 6 explains. Even death will not prevent the Christian from receiving his vindication.

Some Christians known to Peter have died. But the gospel was preached to them during their lifetime. They may well have received rough treatment from their pagan acquaintances. Some (like Stephen) had been killed. In the eyes of the pagans they were thought to be full of superstition, as followers of a crucified Saviour. Their death seemed to be a kind of judgement upon them.

Nothing in 1 Peter teaches that the gospel is preached to any human being after death. Peter does not say 'The gospel **is** preached to those who **have** died'. He says 'The gospel **was** preached to those who **are** dead'. It means that many people have had the gospel preached to them, but since that time have died. Their pagan neighbours thought that this meant they were just like everyone else – that the Christians' 'eternal life' had not prevented them from dying!

The Christians were facing the scoffing and slander of their pagan acquaintances. Peter says to his friends: you may find that your old friends are so astonished by the change that has taken place in your life that they start persecuting you. They may say 'What is the value of this "eternal life" you talk about? You die like everyone else!' But although slandered and condemned by men and women, these Christians will be raised to honour and glory. While in the weakness of a human nature our onetime friends may ridicule and condemn us, but God will have the last word. We Christians will be vindicated and recompensed for every word of slander we have endured. Christ had been preached to us and we have responded in faith and are committed to a new life of godliness, a life of separation from old habits. One day our slanderers will be rebuked; all who have lived for Jesus will be rewarded and will enjoy the resurrection life of Jesus for ever.

Chapter 27

Living in the Endtimes
(1 Peter 4:7–9)

1 Peter 4:7–11 still has in mind the theme of suffering that was introduced in 3:13. Peter has told his friends how to face injustice and how to be encouraged by the triumph of Jesus over all evil forces (3:13–22). He has shown them how suffering helps us to make a break with sin (4:1–6) and ended by pointing to the day when believing people will enjoy the resurrection life of Jesus forever.

Now for a few verses he gives some sharp and short exhortations to these Christians (4:7–11) before coming back to the subject of suffering again (in 4:12).

1. **He points to the nearness of 'the end'.** The Bible is constantly telling us that the end of the world is near. 1 Peter 4:7 begins: *'The end of all things is near'*. This might well puzzle us. How can the Bible say repeatedly even hundred of years **before** Jesus came that the end of the world is near? The answer seems to be that 'the end' is not the final date in the calendar – for that might not be near at all – but the readiness of God to break into our situation. In the Old Testament great crises were regarded as 'the day of the Lord'. They were previews of the end of the world. 'The end is coming on the four corners of the land', said Ezekiel (7:2). In this sense 'the end' is always near. God is near at hand at any point to end **our** world if not to end **the** world. In a time of suffering we need to know God's nearness in this sense.

The persecuted Christian can know that 'the end' is near. In one way or another God is about to break into his predicament.

2. **Peter points to the need for prayer**. Peter is still giving instructions that relate to opposition and persecution. *'Think clearly therefore and give attention to prayers'* (4:7b). He asks them to 'think clearly' or 'be sober'. The Christian is not to be a person who acts on impulse. Peter wants them to clearly think about this matter so that they are men and women controlled by principle and by godly habits. It is not to be a matter of 'When the Spirit leads me, I'll pray' – although that is a good principle in itself! – but there is to be something steadier than that, something more orderly, methodical, deliberate. 'Be sober' says Peter. Give thought to this matter.

How vital it is to pray! What mistakes we shall make if we fail at this point! Who can stand amidst persecutions without prayer? Amidst trials and troubles and oppositions it is prayer more than anything else that keeps our heads cool, that keeps our attitudes free of resentment and bitterness, that enables us to control our tongues.

Prayer is the very essence of knowing God. I do not mean 'saying prayers'. I do not mean following traditional patterns, whether they are catholic-like patterns of formally recited 'prayers' or pentecostal-like patterns of letting the tongue loose to utter anything. I do not mean following traditional patterns at all – of any kind! Prayer is not getting into a mindless routine – of any kind! I refer to talking to God as a Father and friend, turning our minds to Him, getting a conscious realisation that we are in His presence, and then addressing ourselves to Him in worship (verbally expressed joy and admiration of what He is like), thanksgiving (gratitude for what He does every day and what He has specially done for us recently), confession (admitting what He has said to us about our sins), petition (requests for what we need in order to grow in godliness and achieve His will for our lives), or intercession (requests for the need of others). These five ingredients will give us the 'headings' of what we want to talk about with God. **Worship** is adoring His character, recognizing His greatness. **Thanksgiving** is appreciating His generosity, responding to His goodness. **Confession** is admitting our accountability, repenting over our sinfulness. **Intercession** is appealing on behalf of others, requesting for those known to us. **Petition** is asking for mercy and revealing our personal needs. Give attention to prayers!

3. **It is necessary for them to maintain love towards one another** (4:8). Peter could have thought of hundreds of ways to advise his friend in times of conflict and persecution. But he puts it all in a few vital exhortations. It was inevitable that he should ask them to show love towards each other. *'Above all love each other deeply, because love covers a multitude of sins'* (4:8). As always, the Bible incorporates hundreds of things that could be said by putting it in one all-embracing principle: love each other deeply. Then he adds a few words: 'because love covers a multitude of sins'. It is one of those short simple phrases that can be taken in more than way one. Does it mean 'God is merciful to those whom he sees showing love'? Does it mean 'Love does not expose the sins of others but wants them dealt with without disgracing the other person'? Does it mean that the love of God among His people will obliterate sins of aggressiveness among them? It means all of these things and more! Love brings down the mercy of God upon us. Love does not want others exposed. Love works at removing barriers between people.

4. **Peter adds a very practical point: the need for hospitality**. It is a way of making love very practical. The ancient world did not have the kind of 'hotels' that Christians would want to stay in. Peter says: *'Offer hospitality to one another without grumbling'* (4:9). Freedom from a complaining spirit when others require our time and our attention is one way in which the reality of our love is tested.

Chapter 28

Ministering With God-Given Strength
(1 Peter 4:10–11)

Peter is giving a string of sharp and short exhortations to his persecuted Christian friends in Roman Asia Minor, telling them how they should live while they are awaiting God's intervention into their predicament. 'The end' is always near. They need to be steady in their praying. They must maintain love towards one another, not least in practising hospitality.

Now there is one more thing. The Christians should be ministering to each other; God has given spiritual gifts to enable us to do so.

1. **Christians are given gifts of ministry**. Peter implies that every Christian has a spiritual gift of some kind; no Christian is totally lacking in spiritual giftedness. *'Let each person, in the way that he or she has received a gift, use it for the other people, as good stewards of God's varied grace'* (4:10). A gift is any ability experienced in unusual degree that God gives to us by the Holy Spirit for benefiting his church. Every Christian has a spiritual gift.

2. **Gifts of ministry are not to be used selfishly but for the sake of others**. It is easy for certain gifted people to use their gifts for themselves, for their own fulfilment, for getting praise and appreciation from others. Using one's gift is generally enjoyable, so many are tempted to use their gift simply for the sheer pleasure of doing so.

But Peter says 'Let each person ... use it for the other people'. This means our gifts have to be brought under control. We do not use them simply for the joy of doing so.

98

We restrain ourselves and control ourselves to ensure that the gift we have really is doing some good in the church. Joseph in the Old Testament at one stage was using his gift simply for himself (Genesis 37:5–11). Preachers enjoy preaching; administrators enjoy organising; singers like singing. But the question is: do we truly love the people for whom we are using our gift? Or are we simply enjoying ourselves and using others to do so?

3. **Gifts are very varied**. There are many 'spiritual gifts' mentioned in Romans 12:6–8, 1 Corinthians 12:7–11, 28–30; 14:1, 13, 39; Ephesians 4:11; 1 Peter 4:10. Even this is not a complete list and it is possible to think of gifts that are not specially mentioned in the Bible **as gifts** at all (singing or hospitality for example). Even a single gift varies a great deal among different people who have the gift. No two preachers are alike. No two church administrators are alike. Peter says 'Let each person, in the way that he or she has received a gift, use it . . .'. Each gift must be used in the way it has been given. Each person must be himself in the use of the gifts God has given him.

4. **Gifts fall into two categories**. Each person must use the gifts they have as stewards of God's varied grace. *'Whoever speaks should do so as one who utters oracles of God. Whoever serves . . .'*. Peter divides gifts into two categories: speaking and serving. By 'speaking' he has in mind such things as exhortation, teaching, prophesying. By 'service' he has in mind such matters as gifts of administration, of showing mercy, gifts of helpfulness, gifts of giving.

5. **Gifts of speaking should bring the church oracles from God**. There are two types of giftedness. The one who has a gift of speaking of some kind should use his gift 'as one who utters oracles of God'. In other words, the person with the gift of speaking should be sure to use his gift in such a way that what he says is truly a message from God, both in its content and in its timing. His speaking should be a form of the word of God, for the people.

In 'inspired' speaking, the level of inspiration will vary. No Christian today can add to Scripture, or present new doctrines, or ask that his words should be received without testing. No one can speak words from God that are on an equal level with Scripture. 'Speakers' need to have their words tested. In Berea the words even of an apostle were examined 'to see if these things were so' (Acts 17:11).

In Scripture the 'oracles' (inspired messages) were given under the leading of the Holy Spirit and had a God-given relevance to the needs of the people. No one today can speak new doctrines, or claim to have the authority of Scripture, but one can look to God to say what is exactly right for the people. One can look to God to be given exactly the right words.

6. **Gifts of service should be done with God-given strength**. *'Whoever serves should do so out of the strength that God supplies... '.* All ministries need God-given strength, but Peter mentions this in connection with gifts that may be especially tiring. 'Service' – including administration, hospitality, the conduct of worship, settling disputes, ministering to the needy – will often require special strength. The Christian should not try to draw purely on his own strength; he or she should look for additional strength from above.

7. **Gifts of speaking and of service should bring glory to God**. Peter wants every message and every piece of service done with God-given strength to bring about admiration of God. He continues: ' ... *so that in all things God may be glorified through Jesus Christ, to whom belongs the glory and dominion for ever and ever. Amen'.* The reason why God should be admired and our ministries should bring admiration of God is that 'the glory' is His already. He already has a radiant shining character that the Bible calls 'the glory' of God. He already rules over everything. When God gets glorified it is simply a matter of what He is, becoming more widely known, more deeply appreciated. This is what all ministries should do: they should bring God to be more widely known and more deeply appreciated.

Chapter 29

Suffering for the Name of Jesus
(1 Peter 4:12–16)

The last words of 1 Peter 4:11 ('...to whom belongs the glory and dominion for ever and ever. Amen') almost sounded like the end of the letter. What happened was that Peter was led away by the flow of his thought into a slight digression and allowed his treatment of suffering (3:13 to 4:6) to shade off into appeals for godly living during such difficult times (4:7–11). So he ends the digression with an ascription of glory to God, and restarts his teaching about suffering (4:12–19).

1. **They should not be surprised at troubles and tribulations**. We Christians always seem to be surprised when troubles come. 'Surely this ought not to be happening to me!' is our feeling. Actually the very opposite is the case. *'Beloved, do not be surprised at the fiery ordeal that is coming among you to test you, as though something strange were happening to you...'* (4:12). We have been told very clearly that it is 'by means of many tribulations' that we shall enter into an experience of God's kingdom. We actually need some troubles to bring us to be everything that we ought to be for God. This is why Peter says they come 'if it is necessary' (1:6). It has been granted to us – as an act of God's generosity! – to suffer for Christ's sake (Philippians 1:29). We should never be surprised by troubles.

2. **He urges them to rejoice in sufferings**. This is a common theme in the New Testament. James and Paul say much the same thing (see James 1:2; Romans 5:3); and the early Christians really did rejoice in suffering (see Acts 5:41 – in

which Peter was involved). Now Peter says the same thing. *'Do not be surprised ...* (4:12), *but as you share Christ's sufferings, rejoice, in order that also in the revelation of his glory you may rejoice and be glad'* (4:13).

Of course, the Christian does not exactly rejoice in the trouble itself! We are not expected to enjoy suffering. 'All discipline for the moment seems not to be joyful but sorrowful' (Hebrews 12:11). What we rejoice about is not the trouble itself but the fact that we know what God is doing. 'Consider it all joy ... **knowing** ...' (James 1:2). 'We also rejoice in our tribulations, **knowing**...' (Romans 5:3). There is something that we know! We know that God is taking tough and speedy measures to shape our character and purify our faith. Also – Peter's point here – we know that sharing Christ's sufferings will bring abundance of joy in the day when Jesus comes. We rejoice now knowing that we shall doubly rejoice then. We rejoice at the prospect of rejoicing!

3. **There are special promises for those who suffer for they are associated with Christ**. Peter says: *'If you are ridiculed for the name of Christ, you are blessed! For the Spirit of glory and of God is resting upon you'* (4:14).

It seems that the persecution that was beginning in the days of Peter, in and around Roman Asia Minor, had fixed itself not on any particular crime, but upon the mere fact that some people were claiming Christ as their Saviour. The very word 'Christ' was making pagans angry. Often what rouses the furious animosity of the world is not any particular thing we are doing but the mere fact that out of regard for Jesus we are living a godly life. Somehow it makes them feel horribly guilty.

Think of Jesus. He went around doing good and healing people and teaching them about the kingdom of God. He never did anyone any harm. The ordinary people liked to hear Him. Yet there were some who hated Him, and from the earliest days were looking for ways to get rid of Him. Why? What had He done that made them so bitter? It was simply that His pure and sweet love of God aroused their feelings of guilt. They knew that they were not like Jesus, and that made them angry.

The same thing is likely to happen to the Christian. No matter how sweet-natured we may be, some will dislike our love of God. Our refusal to join in with their sins will make them resentful, and soon we find we are being persecuted just for the very name 'Christ'.

Our sufferings should not be caused by our own crimes! Peter says: *'For none of you must suffer as a murderer or thief or a wrongdoer or as an agitator* (4:15) *but if one suffers as a "Christian", let him not be ashamed, but let him glorify God in that name'* (4:16).

There are special promises for the Christian who suffers for Jesus in this way. 'For the Spirit of glory and of God is resting upon you'. In such a situation we can expect more of the power of the Holy Spirit. He will give us a foretaste of glory. A little of the final rejoicing of heaven will come to us even now.

4. **The persecuted Christian goes on to glorify God**. 'Let him not be ashamed!' says Peter. There is a temptation to be ashamed when we are being badly treated. We tend needlessly to blame ourselves. 'What have I done', we ask ourselves, 'that I should be experiencing such unreasonable treatment? Why is this person endlessly slandering me, criticizing me, looking for ways to twist and misinterpret my every action, refusing to allow me even to finish a sentence in my own defence...?'

Let such a person not be ashamed! Perhaps we have made a few mistakes, but the persecution is far greater than anything that could be explained by a few mistakes on our part. If we suffer as a 'Christian' – because it is known that we belong to 'Christ's people' – then no shame or guilt attaches to that! 'Christian' means 'one of Christ's supporters' just as 'Herodian' (in Peter's day) meant 'one of Herod's supporters'.

We go on trusting God! And we glorify God in that name of 'Christian'.

Chapter 30

Judgement at the House of God
(1 Peter 4:17–19)

'For it is the time for judgement to begin; and it begins at the house of God'. If the flow of Peter's thought is followed, it can be seen that by 'judgement' Peter is referring to what is happening in his own day. He has been writing about suffering. Suffering helps the Christian to break from sin (4:1–6). They are facing a 'fiery ordeal' and are likely to be ridiculed for the name of Christ (4:12–16). These are the thoughts that Peter is explaining when he says 'For it is the time for judgement to begin...'.

1. **The people of God occasionally face purifying judgements**. Peter is developing the idea of the 'fiery trial' (4:12). Peter is building on the Old Testament idea that God's people get specially refined. 'You only have I chosen...' said God to Israel (Amos 3:2), 'therefore I will punish you for all your sins'. The people of God get disciplined for their sins, although for a while the world escapes the fullness of God's judgement. In Ezekiel 9, when God is about to chastise the entire nation of Israel and send the nation to exile in Babylon, God's judgement begins at the temple. Only those who have grieved over the sins of the temple escape the coming judgement (see Ezekiel 9:4–6). God says 'Begin at my sanctuary' (Ezekiel 9:6). God said through Malachi 'He will be like a refiner's fire ... He will purify the Levites ... Then Yahweh will have people who bring offerings in righteousness...' (Malachi 3).

So Peter is not referring to the **final** judgement day. 'Right now in our time', says Peter, 'it is a time when God's people are about to be refined'.

The 'house of God' is the church. Peter has already said (in 2:4–5a) that the church may be pictured as being a spiritual temple, a 'holy building' consisting of living stones built upon a living Saviour.

2. **The enemies of God experience judgement that is final and without remedy**. The judgements upon God's people are temporary, and they are purifying, but the judgements upon the world are different. *'And if it starts with us, what will be the end of those who do not believe the gospel of God?'* (4:17).

The judgement of God's people tends to come swiftly; the judgement of God's enemies tends to be delayed. It is time, says Peter, for judgement to **begin** at the house of God – but elsewhere the judgement will be delayed. The ungodly 'store up wrath for the day of wrath' (see Romans 2:5). But we may get some idea of what will happen to the ungodly from what happens to us. 'If this is what **we** have to endure, what will the **unsaved** have to endure?' asks Peter. If this is just a light, correcting rebuke, what will it be like to face the wrath of God without compassion or limitation?

3. **God's chastening lets the Christian know that he or she has a lot to learn**. There is much maturing that has yet to take place in the lives of each Christian. *'And if the righteous person scarcely is saved, where shall the ungodly and the sinner appear?'* (4:18).

What does it mean that 'the righteous person scarcely is saved'? It must be remembered that salvation takes places in stages. We often are very preoccupied with the first stage. 'We are saved', we say. Yes, it is true, the Christian is 'saved'. But actually that is not the entire story. The Christian is saved, he is being saved, and he shall be saved.

(i) He has been saved. He or she is justified; he is born again; he is clothed with the righteousness of Jesus. The righteousness of God is working in his life.

(ii) He is being saved. God is progressively, day by day, delivering him or her from the power of sin.

(iii) He will be saved. God will raise him from the dead and reward him or her for living for Jesus. His righteousness will

105

be vindicated. Everyone will hear his being honoured by Jesus. His glory will shine out from his resurrected body.

When Peter says 'the righteous person scarcely is saved' he is speaking of the second and third of these stages of salvation. He is 'righteous' already. The first stage has already been passed! That was the easy stage. Believing in Jesus is easy when the Spirit is working in our lives. But Peter is not referring to 'the lost' getting saved; he is referring to 'the righteous' getting saved! The righteous need to be progressively delivered from sinful ways, sinful habits, sinful attitudes that hang over from their old pre-Christian days. The righteous need to lay up treasure in heaven, so that Jesus will one day say 'Well done!' to them. But in **this** sense 'the righteous person scarcely is saved'. Sanctification is a battle. We tend to be slow in learning. That is why we need these purifying judgements. They drive us to God and speed up the process of sanctification. They carry forward our salvation. They drive us to the word of God which makes us grow in salvation (2:2). 'The gate is small and the road is narrow that leads to life, and only a few find it' (Matthew 7:14).

So if the righteous have a battle and have to endure purifying judgements, what hope is there for the unsaved?

4. **Peter encourages suffering believers in persistent faith**. Our task is to make sure we are in God's will and persist in faith. *'Therefore let those who suffer according to God's will, trust their souls to a faithful Creator when they do what is right'* (4:19). God is 'Creator'; He controls everything. He is faithful; we can trust Him. If we persist in doing what is right, we shall hear Jesus say 'Well done!'

Chapter 31

The Shepherds of the Churches

(1 Peter 5:1–2)

'Therefore I exhort the elders among you, I, the fellow-elder and witness of the sufferings of Christ, as well as a partaker in the glory that is to be revealed' (5:1).

1 Peter 4:12–19 leads easily into 5:1–3. One can see a connection between suffering Christians (4:12–19) and instructions to elders (5:1–3), because suffering Christians need pastoral help. Peter shows that he has the connection in mind when he uses the word 'Therefore'.

1. **Christians need the care of 'shepherds'.** Peter speaks of himself as 'I, the fellow-elder and witness of the sufferings of Christ, as well as a partaker in the glory that is to be revealed'. He is still making the point that sufferings are the preliminary to glory. He himself had witnessed some of the sufferings of Jesus, and had been an eye-witness of the glory of God in Jesus at the time of the transfiguration (see 2 Peter 1:16–18 where the point is made that the glory seen in the transfiguration is the same glory that will be revealed at Jesus' Second Coming).

Sufferings-followed-by-glory was the sequence of events in the life of Jesus; a similar sequence of sufferings-followed-by-glory will be experienced by Christians. This is the message that the elders must help the people to understand. *'Be shepherds over the flock'*, says Peter. There is no great change of subject; 1 Peter 5:6–11 will still be speaking of anxieties and sufferings. The elders are addressed as those who will give help to Christians in painfully stressful situations. Christians need the care of 'shepherds', but this is specially so in a time of persecution.

2. **Some people are specially recognized in the churches as elders who will work at shepherding the sheep**. Who are these 'elders' to which Peter refers? Mention is made of them in Acts 11:30; 14:23; 15:2–6, 22–23; 16:4; 20:17; 21:18; 1 Timothy 5:17, 19; Titus 1:5 and James 5:14. At first the leadership of the church was in the hands of the apostles. Then administrators arose (Acts 6:1–6, later they were called 'deacons'). Later still elders arose. They may be called 'elders' or 'presbyters' (the Greek word *presbyteros* means 'elder'), or 'overseers' (Greek *episcopoi*; the word 'bishop' comes from this word) or 'those who preside' (*proistamenoi*) or 'leaders' (*hegoumenoi*) or 'shepherds'. It is obvious from the New Testament that 'church government' was highly flexible and that some men could be in more than one recognised ministry.

Roughly speaking apostles, prophets, evangelists, teachers, pastors were five different kinds of preacher. All of them (when helping lead local churches) might also be known by any of the names already mentioned. Then there were deacons who had special gifts of administration. The deacons were not specially preachers, although at least one of them was also (or later became) a powerful preacher (see Acts 6:5, followed by 6:8–7:59).

It seems that in New Testament times there was a lot of flexibility in all of this. The elders were responsible for the spiritual leadership of the church. All of them were 'shepherds' in a general sense. Some of them were 'shepherds' or 'pastors' in a more special sense. Some of the elders, but not all of them, specially gave themselves to teaching (see 1 Timothy 5:17). This means that some people were not only elders in the local church but were also apostles or prophets or teachers or evangelists – or what Paul had in mind by 'pastor' in Ephesians 4:11 – a preacher more specially gifted in shepherding people. (Ephesians 4:11 is listing different kinds of ministry of **preaching**.) Peter refers to himself as both an elder and an apostle. 'Elder' speaks of ministry within the local church.

'Apostle' refers to a certain type of preaching-and-church-planting ministry. Peter could apply both terms to himself.

3. **Peter calls upon the elders to do the work that God has called them to**. Suffering Christians need help. *'Be shepherds over the flock'* says Peter, *'not by way of compulsion but willingly, as God wishes, not for shameful gain but eagerly* (5:2), *not as exercising lordship over the lots but becoming examples to the flock'* (5:3).

The work of being an elder is that of 'shepherding': assisting Christians who are distressed or spiritually torn and wounded; bringing back sheep who wander off into error or sin; praying with and for those who are sick.

Elders must not be lazy. They must not do their work reluctantly or only when they are under compulsion by pressure from others. Rather they must take a delight in their work.

Elders must not be greedy. The church is often used by people who are greedy for money. God's house can easily be invaded by those who are eager for money. Eventually the elders may start forgetting the nature of their work and focusing on acquiring money and using the churches to do so. This happened in the temple of Jerusalem when eventually the money-makers turned the place into a 'den of thieves' (Mark 11:17). But the elders must do their work eagerly. Even if they receive no salary, no financial gain from what they do, if God has called them, they should be eager to get on with the work – whether they gain financially or not.

This is a special temptation to people in developing countries where many people can barely make a living, or depend on the generosity of friends and relatives. People with dubious motives often see the churches as an easy way of getting employment – but such people have no real interest in the work of a shepherd. A true shepherd will do his work if the salary is nil! He looks to God as his salary-payer. If the congregations are used to help him in this way, so much the better, but his eye is on God, not on the offering basket! Elders must not be domineering. If some elders want an easy life, and others want easy money, others may want to be little popes and enjoy lording it over other people.

Peter calls instead for willingness, eagerness, and exemplary living, where the people follow the example of the elders who lead them.

Chapter 32

Jesus the Chief Shepherd
(1 Peter 5:4–5)

Peter is still speaking to the elders and to different sections of the congregations that are led by them.

1. First comes **a final word to the elders** (5:4). *'And when the Chief Shepherd appears you will obtain the unfading crown of glory'* (5:4). It is the way of the Bible, everywhere, to give us encouragement and incentives towards living the godly life. Peter has warned that elders may be lazy, greedy and inconsistent. Yet he does not abandon such people; neither does he question their salvation. He simply urges them to be willing, eager and contented. Then he puts before them the facts of Jesus' coming and the hope of reward.

Jesus is 'the Chief Shepherd'. God does not ask any elder to do anything that He has not already asked from His own Son. Jesus has been, and still is, the Great Pastor, more so than anyone else ever. He is the 'good shepherd' and has laid down His life for the sheep. Jesus has been all that a pastor should be: sacrificial, wise, tender-hearted, patient, willing, eager, content to do God's will. Jesus has been all of these things to us, many times over. No Christian is totally without a pastor to care for him, because Jesus Himself is the chief pastor who shepherds all of His people. Every pastor has a Pastor.

Soon Jesus will appear, visibly, gloriously, and majestically. When He comes those elders who have done their work willingly, eagerly, with consistency and contentment, will receive their victors' crown. Peter does not say precisely what the crown is. Certainly it is a matter of receiving high praise from Jesus. It is a visible indication (like the victor at an athletics competition) that he has overcome the conflicts and adversities in the way of godly living, and in the way of his ministry. Conquerors' crowns are for those who overcome adversities, obstacles, and sufferings.

2. Next comes **a word to the younger people** (5:5a). He says, *'Likewise, younger men, submit yourselves to the older people ...'* (the Greek word for 'elder' is still used, but now it does not have a technical meaning; it simply means 'older person').

In the Bible old age is respected. Young people – Peter probably has in view people in their twenties and thirties – are asked to submit themselves to the older people. There are some good reasons for this (in addition to the fact that it is God's command). The older people may not have the energy that the younger people have. Also they may get a bit traditional and stuck in their ways. Yet they are still to be respected. They have had years of experience and they know that some of the ideals of the younger ones are simply unrealistic theories that will soon be disproved.

The church will be at its best if there is teamwork between young and not-so-young, with the younger people providing energy and zeal and the older folk providing wise leadership, restraint of wildness, and a cool head when there is opposition.

The church is at its best, not when different groups get on with their own thing, but when different groups contribute their different gifts to the supreme tasks of witnessing to the world and building up the church. Within the team the older folk are to be leaders and guides, but the younger folk are indispensable.

3. Next comes **a word to everyone** (5:5b). *'... and all of you clothe yourselves with humility towards one another ...'* The older folk lead; the younger folk have energy but must stay respectful to others. But everyone is to show humility towards everyone else – as Peter has already said (see 3:8).

The best way to understand humility is simply to consider Jesus. He was conscious of His humility (Matthew 11:29). If He could say 'I am gentle and humble ...', how could He do so without pride? He could do so because for Him, humility was a choice! He knew that in a thousand situations He would choose the pathway of lowliness. He knew He would refuse to be resentful because of insult. He knew He would choose the lowly position. Humility does not contradict the 'sober judgement' of Romans 12:3. It is not pretending to be of little worth or significance. That is just pride! It is rather choosing to be oppressed rather than to oppress, to be despised rather than to despise others, to minister rather than to be ministered to (although to be ministered to may also require humility!) The story of John 13:1–20 is one illustration of humility. It took deliberate lowliness for Jesus to choose to do a servant's work. It took some humility for Peter to allow himself to be served by Jesus (see John 13:8). Peter says: 'clothe yourselves'. The royal robe that the Christian puts on is not the demeanour of a pope or emperor or monarch or dictator. He puts on the deliberate indications that he regards himself as no better than anyone else.

4. There comes **a final word of explanation** (5:5c). Peter continues: '...*because God resists the arrogant person but he gives grace to the humble*' (5:5).

It is a quotation from Proverbs 3:34. This should motivate the Christian towards humility. He will be setting up against God if he or she continues in pride or arrogance. God has a habit of bringing failure into the lives of the proud and defeating their intentions and hopes. 'He has brought down rulers from their thrones', says Luke's Gospel, 'and has exalted those who were humble' (Luke 1:52). Nebuchadnezzar walked around his palace and thought how marvellous he was. The slightest hint of any Nebuchadnezzar-like attitudes will produce disaster. Nebuchadnezzar himself learnt it; he lost what he prided himself on the most, his kingdom and his cleverness (see Daniel 4:29–33). Anyone who likes admiration too much is likely to be humbled.

Chapter 33

Depending on God

(1 Peter 5:6–7)

The quotation from Proverbs 3:34 in 1 Peter 5:5 leads him to tell the Christians how to find the pathway of humility. It is a matter of deliberate self-humiliation.

'Humble yourselves therefore under the mighty hand of God, in order that at the right time he may exalt you (5:6). *Cast all your anxieties upon him, because it matters to him concerning you'* (5:7).

He gives an instruction and a promise, then another instruction and another promise.

1. First comes an instruction: 'Humble yourselves therefore under the mighty hand of God...'.

Humility is a matter of humbling ourselves. There will be hundreds of situations in which we shall find opportunity to do so. Peter's people were suffering some persecution – and it was likely to get worse. No situation provides more opportunities for self-humbling.

Every time there is a quarrel there is opportunity for humility. One can leave aside the quarrel without proving one's point. One can let the other person have the last word.

Every time there is injustice there is an opportunity for humility. One can refuse resentment, one can repay ill-treatment with friendliness and out-going concern.

It is God who provides the opportunities for humility. 'How can I be humble?' we ask. Putting on a disguise of humility is not the answer! Pretending to be nothing and nobody is simply inverted pride – even pride of one's humility!

Actually it is God who provides hundreds of opportunities for humility. He has a habit of putting us in a situation where the way we react leads to pride or to humility. Then we humble ourselves under what He is doing to us. We can try to push ourselves into a place of honour (like the man in Luke 12:8) or we can take the position that has no special honour attached to it. What shall we do? Jesus says: 'Do not sit down in a place of honour'.

2. Next comes a promise: '... *in order that at the right time he may exalt you'* (5:6).

Humility will be rewarded with exaltation. Sooner or later God will say to us, 'Friend, go up higher' and you will be honoured. God's promise helps us when we find ourselves in painfully humiliating circumstances. When it is agonizingly difficult to hold back the sharp word, when the other person is obviously acting in foolishness or hostility but is quite unreasonable, when the persecutor clearly has no intentions of showing any mercy – then we keep quiet and humble ourselves. *'When he was insulted, he did not insult the other person; when he suffered, he did not threaten, but he trusted him who judges justly'* (2:23).

We shall be exalted! But some conditions have to be met. (i) We have to humble ourselves first without the slightest attempt to exalt ourselves. (ii) We have to allow the exaltation come in God's way. Peter says '... that **He** may exalt you'. (iii) We have to let the exaltation come in God's time. It may not come just yet, maybe not even until the judgement seat of Christ. But that should be enough to satisfy us.

3. Next comes another instruction. It is not a new command ('Cast all your anxieties upon him ...') but it links tightly with the previous command: *'Humble yourselves ... in order that ... he may exalt you, casting all your anxieties upon him, because it matters to him concerning you'* (5:7).

Peter sees a link between pride and anxiety, and therefore between humility and deliverance from anxiety. Much of our pride stems from anxiety, so as we humble ourselves, at the same time we are to cast our anxiety upon God.

Why are we proud, selfish and arrogant? Because we are full of self-concern. We have anxieties about ourselves. We becomes distressed over how well our reputation is doing, how much we are getting our own way, how secure we are in our finances and possessions. It is anxiety about such matters that makes us edgy, hostile, boastful. overbearing. So if we are to humble ourselves it is necessary that we find a cure for our self-concern. Peter has the remedy: *'casting all your anxieties upon him'*.

Two words need our special attention: 'casting'. It means 'throwing' (as in Luke 19:35, 'throwing their cloaks on its back'). It speaks of something firm and decisive. We are to utterly refuse self-concern and anxiety, drastically throwing our anxiety into the hands of Jesus. Having done so, we refuse to take it back again!

And Peter says 'all'. All our anxieties are to be surrendered to Him! There is no pathway to humility otherwise. Self-concern will produce pride. Release from anxiety opens up the route to humility.

4. Lastly, there comes another promise, a reassurance: *'since he is concerned about you'* (5:7). At the bottom of all pride is self-concern, and at the bottom of all self-concern is the fear that God is not concerned about us. But amazingly, God is deeply concerned about all of the very things that cause us anxiety. Because of God's greatness and holiness we feel that He cannot really be concerned about us. 'How can the God who is so great bother about me?' we ask. And how can One who is so pure and right, not be vexed and irritated by people like us who are so weak and corrupt? And yet we need have no fears about the matter. He provides for sparrows; He will provide for me. He clothes the flowers of the field; He will clothe me also. Since I am flawed and fallen, He has plans to recreate me. The very things that make me so self-concerned, He makes His concern. He is concerned about my reputation; He wants to give me glory. He is concerned about fulfilment; He wants to satisfy me with His plan for my life. He is concerned about finances and possessions; He wants to meet every need as I do His will. I need not bother about arrogance, for He is committed to me and that satisfies my every concern.

Chapter 34

Guarded by God's Mighty Power
(1 Peter 5:8–11)

Peter has further words of advice to his friends who are on the edge of severe persecution. *'Be sober, be watchful. Your adversary the devil roaring like a lion walks around seeking someone to devour (5:8). Resist him, firm in faith, knowing that the same experience of sufferings are required of your brothers and sisters throughout the world (5:9). And the God of all grace, the one who called you to his eternal glory in Christ, after you have suffered a little, he will himself restore, confirm, strengthen and establish you (5:10). To him is the might for ever and ever. Amen'* (5:11).

1. First, there is a command. *'Be sober, be watchful ... '* The first word (Greek: *nepho*) means to be sober; it is the opposite of being drunk. The second word (Greek: *gregoreo*) means to be wakeful; it is the opposite of being asleep.

The Christian is to be a person who is in control of himself. Although his joyfulness may at times be ecstatic and intoxicated, he is not to be so intoxicated that he loses his thoughtfulness altogether. Unlike the drunk he can walk straight and talk straight.

The Christian is to be a person who is wide awake, like a sentry on guard-duty at night-time. He or she knows that they live in a sinful world, and that he himself is full of foolishness and could make a disastrous blunder if he does not stay awake and watch what he is doing and where he is going. Godliness does not take care of itself. The Christian must be in control of himself and stay wide awake.

2. Next comes an explanation: 'Your adversary the devil roaring like a lion walks around seeking someone to devour' (5:8). The Christian has an enemy. His title is 'the devil' – a word that means accuser or slanderer. Like a lion which creates terror when it roars at its prey, so Satan brings about situations which initially terrify us, so that we are ready to yield immediately. But a Christian who is alert and wakeful knows that the roar is itself deceitful and Satan is not as powerful as he would like to pretend.

Like a lion he wanders around looking for the weakest creature that can be easily devoured, seeking one of the herd which is straying from the rest of its companions, weak or maimed in some way and therefore easily captured. Like a lion his desire is to devour and kill. Alertness and wakefulness are needed.

3. Another command: 'Resist him, firm in faith...' The good news concerning Satan is that he is resistible. He is not as powerful as his roars might suggest. Even a lion can be resisted. (A group of wide-awake wildebeest can chase away a lion! Only sleepy stragglers get devoured!)

The Christian resists Satan first by knowing that he can be resisted. The lion's roar paralyzes its victim, and Satan's roar is the same. But the Christian resists Satan with faith. It means that we simply continue to believe God, no matter how great the lion's roaring may be. We stay cool; we remember God's promises; we stand where we are; we do not run away. And the lion goes away! It is faith that defeats Satan. Faith that what God has told us to do, we can do. Faith in God's protection. Faith in the power of the Holy Spirit within us.

4. An encouragement: '...knowing that the same experience of sufferings are required of your brothers and sisters throughout the world' (5:9). The lion was roaring with special brutality and fearsomeness. Persecution was about to break out. Peter wants his friends to know that what is happening to them is not so unusual. There are Christians all over the world – for Peter that was the Roman empire – and many of them are going through the same kind of troubles that face his friends in Roman Asia Minor.

In troubles and sufferings it is good to know that we are not alone and we are not the first to experience these harrassments from Satan. It has been the story of the people of God for a long time, but there is no way Satan can prevent the progress of the kingdom of God.

5. A promise: 'And the God of all grace, the One who called you to his eternal glory in Christ, after you have suffered a little, He will himself restore, confirm, strengthen and establish you' (5:10).

The trials and testings that come from God – with some help from Satan! – do not go on for ever. They come and go. Amidst the fearful oppositions that may come we stand firm in faith.

We are helped by God's purpose of grace. It was grace that saved us. It will be grace that keeps us. God has called us; He is determined to bring us to glory. Persecution cannot defeat us for long, and does not have to defeat us at all. If we stand firm we shall come out stronger. God will restore us. The persecution will be defeated.

6. So Peter concludes with a 'doxology' – an expression of praise to God: *'To him is the might for ever and ever. Amen'* (5:11). This is really the end of the letter; only a few concluding comments remain (5:12–14). Peter's last word is one of praise and worship to God. It was God who chose us, God who sent a Redeemer to rescue us. It will be God who keeps us. Peter's words are a statement: 'To him **is** the might...'. It is a sheer fact that God is mighty. Peter rejoices to know that this 'might' of God is still at work. The grace that took hold of Peter when he was a fisherman will be with him and his people, and it will be with us who believe in Jesus, until it brings the entire people of God to glory. It will stay with us forever.

Chapter 35

Everlasting Peace
(1 Peter 5:12–14)

Now Peter comes to his concluding words. We see in them some of the characteristics that are needed in the work of God's kingdom.

1. **The ministry of the church requires teamwork**. This is something one constantly notices in the New Testament. Peter explains how he expects to have the help of Silvanus in sending the letter to Pontus, the first of the towns of 1 Peter 1:1. *'Through Silvanus, the faithful brother as I regard him, I have written to you a few words...'* It has been debated whether this means that Silvanus was the bearer of the letter, or whether it means that he was the secretary who helped Peter write his letter. A study of the use of the word 'through' in sentences like these tends to support the view that Silvanus was the bearer of the letter and no more (see 'through the hand of' in Acts 15:22, 23 where Silas is the same as the Silvanus of 1 Peter 5:12). It is quite possible that Peter used a secretary, but it is not likely that the secretary was Silvanus.

Peter commends Silvanus because he was a valued co-worker. He is the same person as 'Silas' mentioned elsewhere in the New Testament (see Acts 15:22–40; 16:19–29; 17:10–15; 18:5; 2 Corinthians 1:19; 1 Thessalonians 1:1; 2 Thessalonians 1:1). Possibly Silvanus would have to expound Peter's letter and Peter wants to assure the Christians in Roman Asia Minor that he is a trustworthy fellow worker. It is part of Christian fellowship to commend other Christian workers when we can.

Peter and Silvanus and others are part of a team. Silvanus was willing to take Peter's letter from Rome to Pontus. When he arrived he might well have to represent Peter and explain the letter further.

2. **The ministry of the church is a ministry of grace**. Peter underlines the theme of his letter. *'I have written to you a few words'* he says, *'exhorting and witnessing that this is the true grace of God. Stand firm in it'* (5:12).

His letter has been a letter of exhortation and encouragement. God's people can easily get discouraged and faint-hearted. They need words of encouragement and exhortation – as we Christians of today do also.

Peter has testified of God's grace. He has spoken of God's gift of new birth and Jesus' saving death upon the cross. He has assured us of God's concern for us. It is grace that people need. There is not much motivation in heavy threat or imposing a multiplicity of regulations. Jesus' burden is easy; His yoke is light. These Christians, who are about to face greater persecution than they have ever known, need to hear about God's grace. It is grace that will sustain them in the trials and troubles that are coming upon them.

The graciousness of God in our lives requires confident faith. 'Stand firm in it!' Peter says. Despite what troubles and trials, what doubts and difficulties may come, stand firm in confident expectation that God's grace will give you all the help you need.

3. **The ministry of the church involves gracious friendliness**. Peter gives greetings from the Christians at Rome *('She* [the church] *who is in Babylon, who is chosen like you, greets you')*. And he gives greetings from Mark who is with him. He says: *'And so does Mark my son'* (5:13). 'Babylon' is a way of speaking of Rome. Peter says 'Babylon' to speak of the paganism and worldliness of the city.

Mark is with Peter, acting as his 'son', his friend and assistant. It might be thought that these greetings are simply formal courtesies and do not require much attention from us. Yet greetings are more important than one might think. When little courtesies are omitted a lot of ill-will and suspicion are created. Little courtesies such as these – a 'hello', a 'good morning' or 'farewell' or a 'Praise God' are little points-of-contact in friendship. They do not seem very important and yet when they are lacking, their absence is noticed. Any person wishing to maintain friendship will take care of the little greetings. Peter does so at the beginning (1:2) and now at the end of his letter. Greetings such as these make 'connections' with people. We soon get 'disconnected' if there are no 'hellos' and 'goodbyes', no 'Good mornings' or 'Good-nights'. Such things seem small but if omitted through a kind of superior spirit or sheer sleepiness in such matters, there will soon be trouble and the people concerned become disconnected. Little courtesies such as these make or mar a friendship, a marriage, or a church. Peter is careful to include them in his letter. And he tells them to pay attention to such matters also: *'Greet one another with the kiss of love'*. Love must be **expressed**! It is no good claiming love for another person if the love is somehow secret or only hinted at! Pride tends to hinder the expression of love even when affection is present, but such pride must be overcome. 'Greet one another with the kiss of love', says Peter. Of course such concerns are partly a matter of culture. Different cultures might expression affection differently, but however it might be done, it should be done! Love must be expressed in elementary salutations and greetings.

Finally comes Peter's own last word – one might call it a final friendly 'disconnecting' until one meets again. *'Peace be to you all, you people in Christ'* (5:14). He wished peace for them at the beginning of his letter (1:2); in the middle of his letter he told them to pursue it (3:11). Now he gives his last greeting; and his final wish for them is for peace. There could be no greater blessing in a time of persecution, and Peter is confident that it is possible to be at peace despite the conflicts and pressure that will come when a fiery trial comes upon them. 'Peace' follows on naturally from the references to grace (5:12) and love (5:14a). Anyone who lives in dependence on God's grace and shows love to God's people is likely to experience God's peace.

Some Facts About 1 Peter

Although academic research lies behind this exposition it makes little attempt to deal with scholarly issues. They may be explored in fuller commentaries. Only the briefest of comments may be allowed here.

Authorship. The letter certainly **claims** to be by Peter (1:1) and if it is not then it is difficult (whatever scholars might say to the contrary) to escape the feeling that someone claiming to be Peter has committed an act of fraud. It is however quite possible that Peter asked someone to write it for him, reviewed it, and then sent it out under his name. Silvanus is often mentioned in this connection. This kind of delegation is quite possible without dishonesty. I have myself done something like this for others, and others have done it for me. Indeed for busy preachers it happens quite often. Someone takes notes of a sermon, gives it to the preacher, and the preacher permits it to go out under his name, maybe with a few improvements where the note-taker made mistakes. Some preachers – but I am not one of them – write all their books this way! But it is doubtful if any Christian would feel that he could send a letter claiming to be from Peter if it has no connection with Peter at all. 1 Peter 5:1 refers to the transfiguration; it would be a gigantic deception if Peter did not write it or have responsibility for its being written.

There is plenty of evidence that from earliest days in the church 1 Peter was known to be by Peter. There is no hint of any dispute over the matter. No one thought the claim to authorship by Peter was pious fiction.

Unity. Some have thought 1 Peter is a composite work. This also is doubtful and I have given my explanation of the feeling we have that Peter is re-starting his letter in 4:12.

Recipients. Since Peter was known to have a ministry to Jews, and since the phrases in 1:2 are very Jewish, was this letter sent only to Jews? The answer is probably: no. Outside of Israel it is doubtful if there were congregations consisting exclusively of Jewish Christians and there is nothing in 1 Peter of interest only to a Jewish sub-section of the congregations of 1:1.

Situation. The persecution referred to in 1:6; 3:13–17; 4:12–19; 5:9 was probably the early days of the Neronian persecution of about AD 66, after the great fire in Rome in July AD 64. However if this is so it was the early stages of that persecution, or a preliminary to it. It was not as severe as it became a year or so later. This dates the letter at about AD 63–64. The places of 1:1 are all in Roman Asia Minor – modern Turkey. The letter was a circular sent to these various places.

Place of origin. Peter was in Rome at the time when the letter was written. I take it that 'Babylon' in 5:13 is a code word for Rome.

1 Peter and baptism. During the twentieth century some scholars have seen 1 Peter as a baptismal sermon or even a baptismal order-of-service. The evidence for this is not strong. Baptism is only mentioned in 3:21. Such theories need not interest us.

Further Reading

There are some excellent commentaries on 1 Peter. Standard commentaries include C.A. Bigg's *Commentary on the Epistles of St Peter and St Jude* (Clark, 1902), E.G. Selwyn's *First Epistle of St Peter* (Macmillan, 1947), Ceslaus Spicq's *Epitres de Saint Pierre* (Gabalda, 1966), J.N.D. Kelly's *Epistles of Peter and of Jude* (Black, 1969) and L. Goppelt's *Der Erste Petrussbrief* (Vandenhoek & Ruprecht, 1978).

More recently D.E. Hiebert's *First Peter* (Moody, 1984), W. Grudem's *First Epistle of Peter* (IVP, 1988), J.R. Michael's *1 Peter* (Word, 1988) and P.H. Davids' *First Epistle of Peter* (Eerdmans, 1990) have made valuable contributions. Also helpful is *A Translator's Handbook on the First Letter of Peter* (by Aricha and Nida, UBS, 1980).

Some well-known commentaries may be neglected! I never enjoyed Beare's commentary (3rd ed, 1970) very much; preachers will get little from it.

Similarly works by E. Best (1971), R.C.H. Lenski, J. Moffatt (1947), R.H. Mounce (1982), Clowney (1988) and B. Reicke (1959), Kistemaker, I.H. Marshall (1991) can be left aside. Stibbs & Walls' *First Epistle...* (Tyndale, 1959) was good for its time and Walls' 'Introduction' is still valuable. C.E.B. Cranfield's small *I & II Peter and Jude* (SCM, 1960) is enjoyable.

More expository works include Robert Leighton's excellent *Commentary on First Peter* (various editions) and John

Brown's two nineteenth century volumes (*Expository Discourses on 1 Peter*, 1848, reprinted Banner of Truth, 1975).

Useful for preachers is A. Nisbet, *1 & 2 Peter* (1658, reprinted Banner of Truth, 1982).

Mention ought to be made of Bo Reicke's *The Disobedient Spirits...: A Study of 1 Pet.III.19...* (1946; reprinted by AMS, New York) and W.J. Dalton's *Christ's Proclamation the Spirits* (Pontifical Biblical Institute, 1965) both of which are very interesting.